Merriest, Blessed Christmas

To: _____

From: _____

This day of _____

Also by Rhonda Rhea

Who Put the Cat in the Fridge? Serving Up Hope and Hilarity Family Style

Turkey Soup for the Soul: Tastes Just Like Chicken

Amusing Grace: Hilarity & Hope in the Everyday Calamity of Motherhood

I'm dreaming of some
white chocolate

Christmas Reflections
with a little holly & a lot of jolly

Rhonda Rhea

Revell
Grand Rapids, Michigan

Published by Fleming H. Revell
a division of Baker Publishing Group
P.O. Box 6287, Grand Rapids, MI 49516-6287
www.revellbooks.com

Printed in the United States of America

Library of Congress Cataloging-in-Publication Data

Rhea, Rhonda
    I'm dreaming of some white chocolate : Christmas reflections with a little holly
    & a lot of jolly / Rhonda Rhea.
       p. cm.
    ISBN 10: 0-8007-3136-0 (pbk.)
    ISBN 978-0-8007-3136-6 (pbk.)
    1. Christmas. 2. Christian women—Religious life. I. Title.
BV45.R49 2006
242'.335—dc22   2006012800

Portions of select chapters in the book are adapted from the author's columns in *HomeLife* magazine (Nashville), *St. Louis MetroVoice*, the *Good News Herald* (St. Louis), and *Christian Family Journal* (Kansas City).

To my own "Santas," alias Mom and Dad,
alias Stan and Camille.
No matter what your aliases or what your budget,
you always made every Christmas magical
when I was growing up.

And to Randy and Gina,
the ideal siblings/partners in crime.
I never could've found all those hidden presents without you.

Contents

Christmas Goodies to Bulk Up Your Spirit, but Not Your Thighs

An Introduction

’Tis the season for squeezing weeks of ulcer-inducing shopping between meetings, parties, and Christmas plays, then following it up with about seventy-two straight hours of gift wrapping. Christmas morning I find myself sitting around the tree with a glazed look and half a roll of tape stuck in my hair.

I stack three stories of gifts in front of each child. Within ten minutes we're up to our eyeballs in wrapping paper. I have five children. That's five three-story gift stacks and about 12,000 yards of wrapping paper. Last year it took us three days to find the cat.

Where's the sleep in heavenly peace? Me? I'm dreaming of a long bubble bath and a pound of white chocolate!

But when we look at the big Christmas picture, we understand that Jesus didn't come into the world so we could enjoy a nice story about a reindeer. He didn't come so that our kids could put on a cute play. He certainly didn't come so that we'd have an excuse to induce thighs that are 97 percent white chocolate. Christ was born so that through his sacrificial death we could be reconciled to a holy God. Emmanuel, "God with us," came to pay our sin debt. Christmas is not for making us overworked and overwhelmed but for celebrating how we have been made overcomers.

The season becomes a real celebration when we learn to rest in the faithful hands of the One who has overcome the world. Guess what we find when we rest in him: peace! Jesus said in John 16:33, "In me you may have peace. . . . I have overcome the world."

So let's have a taste or two of *White Chocolate* throughout the season. It's one way we can guard against leaving out our time in God's Word and prayer during the Christmas hullabaloo. It's in the busyness, when we're making snap decisions and dealing with extra stresses, that we need the wisdom he provides all the more! We can let God's Word help us focus on the Christ of Christmas.

Maybe we can even take the time to stop and smell the poinsettias along the way—and find the cat.

Part 1

Jungle All the Way

Beating the Christmas Busies

Season's Meetings

Focusing on Christ in the Christmas run-around

1

About this time every year I seem to start meeting myself to death. Why do I have to ring in the holiday season by attending this Christmas committee meeting, that planning event, the other essential get-together? I'm "meeting" myself coming and going.

I was scanning a newspaper for Christmas sales the other day when I ran across an ad for the Internet: 100 FREE HOURS! That's it! That's what I want for Christmas! Not the Internet service—just the hours. Just a little glance at my holiday calendar could send those with weaker constitutions into months of therapy. And I'm still trying to decide if I'm one of those with a weaker constitution.

Binder Blender

The calendar is now an alphabet demolition derby in a little binder. All the letters, numbers, and symbols are running together so relentlessly it looks like I accidentally dropped the thing in the blender. Who jam-packed these calendar days with so many activities that I've had to start abbreviating to fit everything in those little squares? Surely it wasn't me. The problem now is that I'm having a hard time deciphering my abbreviations. They're pureed! What in the world did I mean when I wrote LST.D.SCL on the calendar for today? Oh my goodness—tell me that doesn't mean it's the last day of school before Christmas break! I was supposed to meet the kids early! One more meeting through the blender!

Add to the meeting mania the fact that I've got to find something fancy and delicious to take to my husband's staff party. I'll have to squeeze the grocery shopping for my party dish in between all the Christmas shopping. Of course, I've only finished one column of my five-column shopping list. And didn't I promise to help with the props for the kids' Christmas play? How did that sneak up on me? Does anyone know where I can find an all-night myrrh store? (Would you believe there's absolutely no help in the Yellow Pages for that?)

I find myself scoping the calendar again. What's even more frustrating is that I notice abbreviations for the kids' program squeezed into the same day I have a Sunday school get-together (or SN.SCHL.GT, if you'd rather read it in Calendar-ese). How could the program be on the same day as the Sunday school party? And it's the Sunday school get-together I *planned.*

Chestnuts Popping in the Microwave?

Visions of sugarplums? I don't think so. Chestnuts roasting on an open fire? Hardly. There hasn't been a silent night around our place since the season began.

Where can we find one of those Norman Rockwell moments? Even if we can't make room for a chestnut or two roasting on an open fire, it seems we should at least be able to find time for some popcorn popping in the microwave.

What do we do when our holiday gets lost in all the holiday activity? Are you doing the holiday shuffle with me, meeting yourself coming and going . . . and going . . . and going—in Energizer Bunny fashion?

If Christmas has lost some of its wonder, some of its charm, some of its blessed meaning in our hearts, maybe it would be healthy for us to steal a few minutes to sit and ponder what the season is about, how we end up so activity laden and stressed, and what we should do about it.

Why are we so mega-stressed? We're living in the age of "mega." We can hardly buy a fast-food meal without someone tempting us to upgrade to the super-whopping-mega size. It's easy to start believing that to have a socially complete Christmas, we have to super-size our schedules in the same way, adding more and more activities to the packed calendar—adding more, spending more, eating more, *stressing* more.

Before we know it, we can be overdrawn, overweight, and overwhelmed. What's an overachiever to overdo?

Put Down the Calendar and Slowly Step Away

The first step, surprisingly, is backward—stepping back to take a look at the big Christmas picture. Christmas isn't just an excuse to make Grandma's plum pudding recipe. It should stay centered on the birth of our Savior. Didn't we just chat about how Christmas is definitely not designed to make us overworked and overwhelmed? I don't mind saying it over again! Christmas can be a season to celebrate how we've been made overcomers. First John 5:5 says, "Who is he who overcomes the world, but he who believes that Jesus is the Son of God?" (NKJV).

We become overcomers not because of any power we muster up in our own strength. Again, the season becomes a real celebration when we learn to rest in the faithful hands of the One who has overcome the world. Knowing he overcomes and knowing he has made us overcomers brings about that most amazing Christmas gift: peace. Look at what

Jesus said in John 16:33: "These things I have spoken to you, that in Me you may have peace. In the world you will have tribulation; but be of good cheer, I have overcome the world" (NKJV). The Lord is the One who has done the overcoming. He's the One who gives the peace. The only thing we truly need to work for is the resting ability.

Over and Out

So if you're struggling with overdoing and all the other "overs," maybe today is the perfect day to, well . . . get over it! We can find rest in a real Christmas celebration. "Rest" and "merry" go together like turkey and dressing. Even better, they don't make you sleepy an hour later. No sleepiness, just peacefulness. It's no coincidence that the old Christmas carol says: "God rest ye merry, gentlemen, let nothing you dismay / Remember Christ our Savior was born on Christmas Day. . . ."

In all the merry mayhem, it's helpful to remember to be consistent in soaking in the message of the Christ of Christmas every day. That's what will generate true merriment, all wrapped in peace.

I love thinking about that special delivery message brought by the angels at that first Christmas meeting: *Glory to God . . . and on earth peace.* You gotta love a meeting with a message of peace!

I think I'll set my calendar aside for the day and study on the message for a while. And I think I'll use my blender to make a smoothie.

And there were shepherds living out in the fields nearby, keeping watch over their flocks at night. An angel of the Lord appeared to them, and the glory of the Lord shone around them, and they were terrified. But the angel said to them, "Do not be afraid. I bring you good news of great joy that will be for all the people. Today in the town of David a Savior has been born to you; he is Christ the Lord. This will be a sign to you: You will find a baby wrapped in cloths and lying in a manger."

Suddenly a great company of the heavenly host appeared with the angel, praising God and saying,

"Glory to God in the highest,
and on earth peace to men on whom his favor rests."

Luke 2:8–14

Christmas Shoes   2
Stepping into a redeeming Christmas

I have my own version of the Christmas Shoes story. It was a Sunday near Christmas and I had donned my nicest gay (happy) apparel. I was wearing exceptionally cute shoes. That's important to note since cute shoes are so integral to that classy Christmas look. The problem with cute shoes is that they're so seldom practical. I can't remember a single time anyone has said to me, "Would you take a look at my adorable orthopedic shoes!" "Cute" usually means painful. Sometimes it even means dangerous.

The Sunday I was sporting the exceptionally cute shoes is a good example. I was walking down the hallway at church looking ever so fashionable, when one of the attractive high heels made an unexpected forty-five-degree turn to the west. The rest of me took on a new course heading due south. Maybe if it had been a few degrees less I could've pulled out at the last minute. Sadly, I knew instinctively that forty-five degrees is past the point of no return. Picture an overloaded sleigh without its full complement of reindeer. I was going down.

Shoe Fly

You can try it, but I can tell you it's not going to work. Try to look graceful and charming and hang on to that look of holiday class when you're taking a nosedive in the middle of the church hallway. In a dress.

I tried to bounce up with an "I *so* meant to do that," but no one was buying it.

I was relieved that at least we were between rush hours in the church hall. I only humiliated myself in front of a handful of people. And such godly people they were. I really have to give them credit. They were trying to look sincerely concerned—right before they exploded into uncontrolled laughter. I thought I was going to have to give one of them a little CPR. I hate it when I make my friends swallow their gum.

By the way, it doesn't matter how cute the Christmas shoes are, they just don't give you that runway look when they end up flying through the air. It's amazing how things can take a bad turn so quickly.

Step into the Light

Those bad turns can pop up in every area of life. That's the reason we have to be especially careful. Ephesians 5:15–17 says, "So watch your step. Use your head. Make the most of every chance you get. These are desperate times! Don't live carelessly, unthinkingly. Make sure you understand what the Master wants" (MSG).

Watching our step doesn't necessarily mean always wearing sensible shoes. But it does mean we need to guard our thinking and our actions. The New King James Version puts Ephesians 5:15–17 like this: "See then that you walk circumspectly, not as fools but as wise, redeeming the time, because the days are evil. Therefore do not be unwise, but understand what the will of the Lord is."

Redeeming the time. That's our calling. When I was a little girl, my grandmother collected Green Stamps. I remember thinking how magical it seemed one Christmas season when Grandma took a few stamp-filled books to the redemption center and traded them for the most wonderful fashion model doll for me. (Incidentally, the doll had the cutest high heels I had ever seen, which is probably what kicked off, so to speak, my cute-shoe need.) But I've never forgotten the almost enchanted way my grandmother redeemed those stamps for something that was of great value to me. It was like trading for treasure!

I want to redeem my time—and redeem my Christmas season—in the same way. I want to exchange my time, even in the busiest season, for something of great value to my Savior. I want to make it something that I can treasure, and something that he treasures. I want to celebrate his birth in a way that will bless, glorify, and honor the Savior.

Look Out

Spending too much time on a "look" is not redeeming my time. It's not making the most of every opportunity to live for Christ. Living "carelessly" and "unthinkingly" is so much more dangerous than sporting the cutest pair of shoes. It results in a Christmas—and an entire lifetime—spent in fruitlessness. We need to forget the runway and "understand what the Master wants."

We find what he wants by focusing on him. We find what he wants by staying persistent in prayer. We even find what he wants by studying his Word. There's direction in the Word of God that will never send us spiraling out of control. No unexpected south turns there! It's the secure life—the clean life. Psalm 119:9 says, "How can a young person live a clean life? By carefully reading the map of your Word" (MSG).

If you've been spiraling out of control or quietly heading down the wrong runway, it's time to dust yourself off and change direction. Head God-ward. Follow his map for living and your steps will be steady. Psalm 119:5–8 says, "Oh, that my steps might be steady, keeping to the course you set; Then I'd never have any regrets in comparing my life with your counsel. I thank you for speaking straight from your heart; I learn the pattern of your righteous ways. I'm going to do what you tell me to do" (MSG).

You'll find joy in a wonderful place of no regrets when you're obediently following his instructions. Great joy. Even in orthopedic shoes.

Therefore, prepare your minds for action; be self-controlled; set your hope fully on the grace to be given you when Jesus Christ is revealed. As obedient children, do not conform to the evil desires you had when you lived in ignorance. But just as he who called you is holy, so be holy in all you do; for it is written: "Be holy, because I am holy."

Since you call on a Father who judges each man's work impartially, live your lives as strangers here in reverent fear. For you know that it was not with perishable things such as silver or gold that you were redeemed from the empty way of life handed down to you from your forefathers, but with the precious blood of Christ, a lamb without blemish or defect. He was chosen before the creation of the world, but was revealed in these last times for your sake. Through him you believe in God, who raised him from the dead and glorified him, and so your faith and hope are in God.

1 Peter 1:13–21

Overseasoning the Season   3
Dealing with the indigestion-inducing busyness of a spicy season

One more of those little sausages and I might drown myself in barbecue sauce and leap into the Crock-Pot. I've had so many this season that I see them in my sleep. It's not nearly as pleasant as dreaming of white chocolate. I am officially oversausaged. I'm not the only one. At the last party I noticed one of the guests slipping them to our cat under the table. I just shrugged and slipped him a couple more. Sammy's having a great Christmas.

If only I didn't wait to decide I've had too many sausages until . . . well . . . I've had too many sausages, if you know what I mean. Sixteen thousand calories later, I figure it out. The revelation becomes complete in January when I'm trying to zip my favorite jeans. Then there is weeping and wailing and trashing of jeans.

I heard one wife complain that she knows the holiday overeating season is just about complete when she has to dial 911. She said the paramedics usually have to use the Jaws of Life to get her husband out of his recliner.

What a season! So much food. So little room in the jeans.

I thought it might be helpful if I made a checklist with the top ten overeating signs for those of us who spice up our season with a few too many calories. Any time we have to check off more than a couple of these items, it might be a good idea to ask for a health club membership for Christmas.

Top Ten Signs Your Holiday Overeating Is Out of Control

10. You hunt for a turkey that's bigger than a Volkswagen.
 9. You decide that the only gravy boat that goes with a VW-sized turkey is your husband's twelve-foot bass boat.
 8. Your doctor decides you'd better get a cholesterol screening, but the finger prick yields cranberry sauce.
 7. You realize the red stripe on your belly is actually steering wheel burn.
 6. Your family invites Jenny Craig over—for your intervention.
 5. Jenny asks you to be her poster child.
 4. You're inducted into The Little Smokie Hall of Fame.
 3. Your husband gives you an extra-long strand of pearls for Christmas, but you can't swallow when you wear them.

2. You drop a turkey leg on your belly while having a snack—and you never find it.

1. You notice you're being orbited by a small moon.

Personally, I try to get a handle on overeating sometime before I notice the moon. That gravitational pull does such a number on my holiday hairdo.

Isn't it amazing how our schedules can get "overseasoned" too?

How Do You Spell Relief? K-I-N-G-D-O-M T-H-I-N-K-I-N-G

Activity-indigestion resulting from an overly spicy Christmas season can be relieved as we make sure we're committed to genuinely worthy activities. Busyness isn't condemned. It's actually encouraged—even commanded. But empty, fruitless busyness is an even sadder waste than little sausages slipped to an already overweight cat.

It's so easy to get our priorities mixed up when life is too busy. We tend to overindulge in the temporary and starve ourselves of the eternal. Talk about a spiritual diet out of balance!

We find perspective when we trade empty busyness for kingdom busyness. Let's make sure the things we're in a flurry over are the things that count in the kingdom—the things that count eternally. Second Timothy 2:1–7 says,

> So, my son, throw yourself into this work for Christ. Pass on what you heard from me—the whole congregation saying Amen!—to reliable leaders who are competent to teach others. When the going gets rough, take it on the chin with the rest of us, the way Jesus did. A soldier on duty doesn't get caught up in making deals at the marketplace. He concentrates on carrying out orders. An athlete who refuses to play by the rules will never get anywhere. It's the diligent farmer who gets the produce. Think it over. God will make it all plain. (MSG)

The Kingdom Fruit Diet

Throwing ourselves into the kingdom work of Christ means saying no to those frivolous, fruitless works. We're instructed to say a giant yes to the kingdom work just as a soldier says a "yes, sir!" to his commanding officer, and as an athlete responds in obedience to the rules laid out by the coach. If we want fruit instead of barrenness, then we have to be as diligent as a faithful farmer. In verse 15, we're further reminded to "concentrate on doing your best for God, work you won't be ashamed of, laying out the truth plain and simple" (MSG).

Having to be pried out of the La-Z-Boy with the Jaws of Life would be pretty embarrassing—not exactly something any of us would like to be remembered for. But doing our best in our kingdom work for God means not having to be ashamed.

Will there still be little, nitty-gritty, seemingly unimportant activities crowding the Christmas to-do list? I'm afraid so. But as we sift our busyness through kingdom thinking, we're able to immediately spot more of the activities that are wholly in the non-kingdom category. We can trim some of that holiday fat and focus on the true reason for the season: Jesus. As we cut some of the busyness, we find more time for serving him and sharing his love with those around us.

So when that indigestion starts to set in and we're overstuffed with fruitless holiday worries, let's not allow those worries to crowd out our work for Christ. More kingdom work—fewer sausages.

Do you see what this means—all these pioneers who blazed the way, all these veterans cheering us on? It means we'd better get on with it. Strip down, start running—and never quit! No extra spiritual fat, no parasitic sins. Keep your eyes on Jesus, who both began and finished this race we're in. Study how he did it. Because he never lost sight of where he was headed—that exhilarating finish in and with God—he could put up with anything along the way: cross, shame, whatever. And now he's there, in the place of honor, right alongside God. When you find yourselves flagging in your faith, go over that story again, item by item, that long litany of hostility he plowed through. That will shoot adrenaline into your souls!

Hebrews 12:1–3 MSG

Making a List and Stressing Over It Twice

4

Exchanging Christmas stresses for a few more fa-la-la's

It's amazing how the Christmas season, so swiftly yet stealthily, can become more like a gigantic, overwhelming to-do list than a celebrative holiday. The "merry" of the season slinks away, covered over in a flurry of frenzy and a large jug of one of those stomach-coating medicines.

There's plenty of stress, but not so much genuine "fa-la-la-la-la," if you know what I mean. The familiar lyrics of "Deck the Halls" take on a new yuletide twist:

> Stomach walls need much Mylanta
> Fa-la-la-la-la, la-la-la-la
> Kids are focusing on Santa
> Fa-la-la-la-la, la-la-la-la
> Stressing out to plan the party
> Fa-la-la, la-la-la-la-la-la
> Chug the Pepto by the quarty
> Fa-la-la-la-la, la-la-la-la

Just making the giant to-do list can be pretty stressful, even before checking it twice. How many miles of fake greenery will it take to make that loopy-looking thing happen across the front porch? Did we make sure our porch is at least as green as the neighbor's porch? And don't we need to hang Christmas wallpaper before the open house?

That deco-to-do list is stacked on top of the shopping list. Oh, the shopping! Not only do I need to make sure I've been to every major store to buy for the list of aunts, uncles, cousins, hairdressers, and postal workers. There's more. I then have to go back around to the layaway departments of all the major stores and make sure there aren't any other list items I've tucked away and forgotten. I guess it's just a little too easy to lay it too far away.

All-Night Card Party

It gets all the more overwhelming when you have to add another list to the already radioactive list of lists. It's the Christmas card list, and before you know it, you find yourself doing that Christmas card shuffle again. Most of us usually wait until the very last minute, then try to address and stamp at hummingbird velocity—cards flying left and right as we're praying for paper-cut protection.

Have you ever made it to bed in the wee hours of the morning after the Christmas-card-a-thon only to find you couldn't sleep? The disgusting taste of lingering envelope glue is too distracting. It's even worse when you wake up the next morning to find your tongue bonded to the roof of your mouth. I'd tell you more, but these lips are sealed.

It's pretty typical to end up massaging our collective temples with an empty cardboard Christmas paper roll, as the overwhelming to-do list runs through our pounding heads one more time. How does the craziness sneak up on us and replace our season of celebration and jubilation with a season of mega-complication and stomach medication?

The Ultimate Layaway

There's a better, nonmedicated way to go. Psalm 4:6–8 says, "Why is everyone hungry for more? 'More, more,' they say. 'More, more.' I have God's more-than-enough, more joy in one ordinary day than they get in all their shopping sprees. At day's end I'm ready for sound sleep, for you, God, have put my life back together" (MSG).

In Matthew 6:19–20, Jesus himself reminds us of the ultimate layaway plan. "Do not lay up for yourselves treasures on earth, where moth and rust destroy and where thieves break in and steal; but lay up for yourselves treasures in heaven, where neither moth nor rust destroys and where thieves do not break in and steal" (NKJV).

Heavenly layaways are never forgotten. They never rust, never get stolen—never get spoiled by rogue envelope glue. Christ's kind of layaway is all about the heart: "For where your treasure is, there your heart will be also" (v. 21 NKJV).

Knowing that our real treasure is wrapped up in Christ in a heavenly anti-theft, anti-rust zone puts our overwhelming earthly lists in perspective—and quite frankly, it helps us understand that some of the things on our lists are frivolous stress enhancers. Understanding real treasure can make for a few less antacids as we're instead overwhelmed by his hope.

Hebrews 10:22–23 says, "Let us draw near with a true heart in full assurance of faith, our hearts sprinkled clean from an evil conscience and our bodies washed in pure water. Let us hold on to the confession of our hope without wavering, for He who promised is faithful" (HCSB).

Christmas to the Fullest

That's heart treasure! Because Christ came to earth in flesh, forgiveness is available to all. It's the heart-sprinkling, sin-cleansing, hope-giving blood of Christ that can put an end to empty list-mania and replace the empty life with life to the fullest.

"For you know that you were redeemed from your empty way of life inherited from the fathers, not with perishable things, like silver or gold, but with the precious blood of Christ, like that of a lamb without defect or blemish" (1 Peter 1:18–19 HCSB). Now there's what we need—a full season. Really. We need a season full of jubilant celebration of the Lamb!

That's my goal. It's going on the top of my list: Sweat less. Treasure more—in the sincerest, most joyful fa-la-la fashion.

When I do happen to sweat, I think at least it might help me with the decorating. After all those envelopes, I'll probably be sweating wallpaper paste.

Don't hoard treasure down here where it gets eaten by moths and corroded by rust or—worse!—stolen by burglars. Stockpile treasure in heaven, where it's safe from moth and rust and burglars. It's obvious, isn't it? The place where your treasure is, is the place you will most want to be, and end up being.

Your eyes are windows into your body. If you open your eyes wide in wonder and belief, your body fills up with light.

Matthew 6:19–22 MSG

Ho-Ho-Hold It!   5
How to keep from getting a holiday he-he-headache

It's easy to get fed up with all the busyness during this season, isn't it? It seems almost every time I'm out shopping and running errands (yes, nearly every day from November 1 through December

24), I end up out of time and driving through for a fast-food burger for lunch. By dinner I'm still doing the maniac routine, and I'm rolling my eyes as I roll through the drive-through for burgers to take home to my family for dinner. And it's the third burger night in one week. Am I the only one starting to look entirely too much like Santa? Argh, I'm looking like Santa but feeling more like one of his reindeer. Somebody please stop me before I ask for a salt lick for Christmas.

It's a Line Drive

One day last week (right before I drove through for yet another burger), I found myself standing in the checkout line to beat all checkout lines. This thing wrapped around the store three or four times. I had already been through several lines in several other stores and a post office line that could've made anyone go postal.

I looked around at all the cattle-folks in the latest herd with me. It worried me that I was starting to feel much too comfortable in the checkout roundup. Since eating all those burgers, I've surely got to be at least one-quarter cow by now. I decided to break the burger-thon and get a fast-food salad. Did that settle my livestock worries? Oh no. I then got a little worried that maybe I had so overly beefed myself that I was starting to graze. All the worrying just gave me one more big, beefy headache. The whole thing did very little to get me into the Christmas moo-oo-ood.

Got aspirin?

Honestly, if I have to drive through for one more hamburger, I think it might send me into a long-term humbug mode. Can I get a "hum-bugger" to go?

Would You Like Fries with That?

All farm animals and fast food aside, unless we want to end up making a trip to the doctor (or the vet) for some moo-oo-ood meds, we need to slow down some of the drive-through madness. Before we polish off the entire bottle of Excedrin, we need to put on the brakes and de-busy the schedule. Take a look at the practical side and try a few headache-relieving busy-beaters.

Feeling you have to tackle it all by yourself, for instance, will add to your stress big-time. Try sharing some of the pickup and deliveries with your spouse, your kids, or some other willing victim — er . . . helper . . . whenever you can. Share some of the shopping list too. We all need to send out an S.O.S. (Save Our Sanity) at some time or another.

If you don't have a spouse who can help out, maybe a relative or friend would be willing to help. Or if the budget allows, try hiring out some of those tasks until the flurry of activity dies down. Hiring out that laundry might be a great stress-relieving Christmas gift to yourself. If you can afford a housekeeper for a couple of months, take advantage of that, and let it help you through the busy season.

Setting a reasonable schedule and some reasonable goals will help with the stress level. If you list your activities and then prioritize them, you might find some things you can cut or a few things that can wait until the busyness dies down.

Entering major stress mode is a sign that instead of super-sizing, it's time for some simple-sizing. Take an objective look at what is doable and what isn't. Where can you simplify? If there are items on your schedule that just don't fit, you may even need to decline a few invitations. If you do, go ahead and decline — without the guilt. Understand that you can't do it all. And that's okay. Say a few no's with a humble apology and folks will almost always understand. Chances are they're sinking in the Christmas flood of activity too. You may have to adopt a new slogan for a while: Just Un-do It.

Order Up a Little Solitude

It's easy to forget that we need some solitude now and then. It's tough to force ourselves to get alone and be still for a few minutes when the flurry of lists tugs at our adrenal glands. But there is great perspective in solitude and stillness. Go ahead. Put solitude — a little stillness — on your Christmas to-do list. It can help you guard against the fatigue that will steal the energy you need to accomplish those things you have to do anyway.

We have to be careful, too, that we don't let doing things for our family drown out time with our family. If you find you need to make a few changes, don't cower away from them. (Did I really just say "COW-er"?)

All beefy drive-throughs and long lines considered, Jesus needs to stay in the number one spot on our list of priorities. Isn't it sad when we leave him out of his own birthday celebration? Make time to soak in some Jesus. Invite him into your way of thinking. That will make all the difference in keeping a bright, right focus amid a lot of holiday insanity. It's the only way to make the holiday a true "holy day," as it's actually meant to be. And it may even save us from a bad case of mad cow disease.

> Are you tired? Worn out? Burned out on religion? Come to me. Get away with me and you'll recover your life. I'll show you how to take a real rest. Walk with me and work with me — watch how I do it. Learn the unforced rhythms of grace. I won't lay anything heavy or ill-fitting on you. Keep company with me and you'll learn to live freely and lightly.
>
> Matthew 11:28–30 MSG

Part 2

Please Have Snow, and Mistletoe, and Presents . . . Lots of Presents

Curbing Materialism

Three More Wishes

6

Answering the "I wanna's" from the Word

here comes a time in every Christmas season when I start to feel like one of my kids' video games. They're busy pushing all my buttons, trying to score all the right gifts. I wonder if they compare scores after Christmas. Do you suppose the one who inspired the biggest dollar amount wins?

What do you do when one wants a Bazooka Bob and a G.I. Junior M-16? That's frightening enough, but who knows where to go to find the Emeril life-size edition Easy-Bake Oven? How about the modeling-clay version of the "Perform Your Own Appendectomy" game? Most of the kids add money somewhere on their list of "I wannas." Lots of money. Just in case there's something they forgot. It's sort of like rubbing the lamp, making two of their wishes, then wishing for three more wishes. What am I, a parent or a genie? Now that I think about it, one of the kids may have asked me one year for an *I Dream of Jeannie* costume.

Where's a Genie When You Need One?

What amazes me is that even after having all my buttons pushed, I find myself fighting traffic, wading through sale tables, sifting through the noise of a thousand parents crying out for the last, lone Gourmet

Easy-Bake. Sounds like a nightmare curse straight from the pages of Ali Baba's story, doesn't it?

In Psalm 27:4, the psalmist wrote about his "wanna." Interestingly, he said, "I'm asking GOD for one thing, only one thing." Asking for only one thing? It's almost absurd, isn't it? Surely this passage isn't meant for Christmas. Didn't he understand that celebrating Christ is almost always followed by a humongous list of wants? One thing? But the psalmist says, "I'm asking GOD for one thing, only one thing: To live with him in his house my whole life long. I'll contemplate his beauty; I'll study at his feet" (Ps. 27:4 MSG).

Wha-da-ya-want for Christmas?

It's easy to get caught up in the lists of wants and the busy noise of the Christmas season and forget who we're celebrating. Christmas is about God's Son coming in human form. He came as a baby, knowing he was destined for the cross. It's the most beautiful story of all time—our redemption. Isn't it sad that it's so easy to get distracted by all the noise and totally miss the beauty?

The next verse in Psalm 27 tells us that contemplating his beauty and studying at his feet is really the only way to beat the noise. "That's the only quiet, secure place in a noisy world, the perfect getaway, far from the buzz of traffic" (v. 5 MSG).

The perfect getaway! What could be better than the promise of living with our magnificent Savior our whole lives long? What could be better than studying at his feet, soaking in his beauty? When we come face-to-face with his glorious beauty, every other temporary treasure in life—even the Bazooka Bobs and life-size Easy-Bakes—everything we've ever seen as a "must have" will suddenly become a "what was I thinking?" We could be bottled up for thousands of years and still find that true satisfaction doesn't come from where we are or what we have, but that it's really about treasuring the right treasure.

We discover great treasure as, amid all the wants, we funnel our kids toward Jesus and to his Word. Maybe it will help if we remind them that his Word is a "lamp" to our feet. Okay, maybe not the genie kind of lamp. But if we can say "open sesame" as we open his Word, we can find new ways to contemplate his beauty. We can find unspeakable family treasure as we're studying at his feet.

Contemplate His Beauty, Study at His Feet

"Contemplating" and "studying" means meditating on him. Psalm 145:3–4 says, "Great is the Lord and most worthy of praise; his greatness no one can fathom. One generation will commend your works to another; they will tell of your mighty acts." One generation teaching the next generation about the greatness of God—sounds a little like Old Testament family devotions, doesn't it?

The psalmist continues: "They will speak of the glorious splendor of your majesty, and I will meditate on your wonderful works" (v. 5).

There's majestic treasure in meditating on him. It's treasure that beats the socks off any genie outfit (though, if I remember correctly, that outfit doesn't actually come with socks). Here's wishing us all a majestically "Meditative Christmas" and a "Highly Fruitful New Year"!

> The LORD is my light and my salvation—
>   whom shall I fear?
> The LORD is the stronghold of my life—
>   of whom shall I be afraid?
> When evil men advance against me
>   to devour my flesh,
> when my enemies and my foes attack me,
>   they will stumble and fall.
> Though an army besiege me,
>   my heart will not fear;

though war break out against me,
    even then will I be confident.
One thing I ask of the LORD,
    this is what I seek:
that I may dwell in the house of the LORD
    all the days of my life,
to gaze upon the beauty of the LORD
    and to seek him in his temple.
For in the day of trouble
    he will keep me safe in his dwelling;
he will hide me in the shelter of his tabernacle
    and set me high upon a rock.
Then my head will be exalted
    above the enemies who surround me;
at his tabernacle will I sacrifice with shouts of joy;
    I will sing and make music to the LORD.
Hear my voice when I call, O LORD;
    be merciful to me and answer me.
My heart says of you, "Seek his face!"
    Your face, LORD, I will seek.

                                    Psalm 27:1–8

May I Take Your Order, Please?   7
Trading a clown-head Christmas for real soul food

I went shopping the day after Thanksgiving last year.
    I was an idiot.
    I found myself trying to maneuver through the electronics
department at the most jam-packed store in the county at 6:00 in the

morning. I was waiting for them to dole out the bargain of the season. It was some electronic game thingy that I knew nothing about—only that it was on one of my kids' Christmas lists.

The real problem was that when they finally did start rationing out the toys, I couldn't lift a hand to snag one. Both arms were pinned down by the dozens of other zombie parents wearing the glazed look that says, "Why am I spending a vacation day coming here in the middle of the night to save twenty bucks on a toy that will be forgotten by February?"

I decided after the shopping trip that I'd happily pay the twenty bucks not to have to go through that again. Would you believe there was a lady at one store who actually passed out in one of the aisles? No kidding! She literally shopped till she dropped!

Dropping the Shopping

I'm a born shopper, but there comes a point in the Christmas buying season that I think I'd happily drop the shopping for life. Okay, maybe not for life. But I'd surely be willing to take an extended vacation from any place where I could hear "Attention, shoppers" echoing from the ceiling.

It doesn't help when my kids have started sort of "placing their orders." They give me their rehearsed speeches, letting me know in no uncertain terms that they want this game, that sweater, and the other CD. When they worry I might not be getting it all, they write it down for me. Isn't that thoughtful?

I even get a computerized list from my son Jordan. He pulls up pictures of what he wants for Christmas, gives me the prices, lists websites or names of stores where I can find each item—he even puts a handy box beside each item so I can check things off as I fill his order. I told him last Christmas that his list made me feel a little like a five-foot catalog wearing Christmas earrings, so he graciously changed his format. Instead of "Jordan's Christmas List" across the top of this year's list, he chose a different font (very attractive, I must say) and titled it, "Buying Guide for Jordan."

Even though the "Christmas list" has been exchanged for a "buying guide," I have a feeling this Christmas is still destined to have a bit of a clown-head feeling. Why don't I just install a drive-up window and let my kids roll through with their requests? *May I take your order, please? Would you like batteries with that?*

What Do We Really Need?

We tend to see so many things in this life as needs, don't we? We work and sweat to make sure we have the homes, cars, clothes, and extra channels that will label us successful people in our society's view.

But in Matthew 16:26, Jesus asks, "For what profit is it to a man if he gains the whole world, and loses his own soul? Or what will a man give in exchange for his soul?" (NKJV).

Wow, what a powerfully soul-probing question. What good is it to work ourselves silly all our lives to make sure we have everything we need, even everything we want, but in the end lose everything—right down to the soul?

Jesus doesn't beat around the bush. He makes it clear that the spiritual is eternally more vital than the physical. So why is it so easy for us to get wrapped up in making a living, buying all the things that sparkle, chasing the dream, finding everything on life's list? We can get so distracted by those temporary things that we neglect, even ignore, the spiritual, eternal side of life.

You Can't Take It with You

Those who do eventually "have it all" find in the end that all those things they've worked so hard for are ultimately lost to them. "You can't take it with you" is true of every item that any child of mine has ever ordered for Christmas. It's true of every pointless thing I've chased after myself. If all a person seeks in this life is in the temporary category, that person will come up empty at the end of life. To lose your soul is to truly lose everything.

You *Can* Take This!

But here's a merry Christmas thought we can take with us. As we trust in Jesus, our soul is ever and always eternally secure. There's some soul food you can really sink your teeth into! No soul is ever, ever lost in Christ. In fact, there's an inheritance in Jesus that makes every big and every little thing we've ever worked for in this life seem like an irritating echo from the ceiling. A glorious inheritance awaits us!

As we humble ourselves and give all to the Savior, we inherit everything—the whole world. Matthew 5:5 says, "God blesses those who are humble. The whole earth belongs to them!" (CEV).

Here's what 1 John 2:15–17 says: "Don't love the world's ways. Don't love the world's goods. Love of the world squeezes out love for the Father. Practically everything that goes on in the world—wanting your own way, wanting everything for yourself, wanting to appear important—has nothing to do with the Father. It just isolates you from him. The world and all its wanting, wanting, wanting is on the way out—but whoever does what God wants is set for eternity" (MSG).

I want to be set for eternity! Lists come and go. Jesus is forever. Did I say "lists"? I meant "buying guides."

In Him also we have obtained an inheritance, being predestined according to the purpose of Him who works all things according to the counsel of His will, that we who first trusted in Christ should be to the praise of His glory.

In Him you also trusted, after you heard the word of truth, the gospel of your salvation; in whom also, having believed, you were sealed with the Holy Spirit of promise, who is the guarantee of our inheritance until the redemption of the purchased possession, to the praise of His glory.

Ephesians 1:11–14 NKJV

All I Want for Christmas

8

Finding joy in the better way

Who would ask for their two front teeth for Christmas? If I'm going to do something cosmetic, I'm aiming for altogether different parts. Can I get dirt-dog honest about what I really want for Christmas? Boy, would I like a new body—or at least a renovation on this one. How many miles do you have to have on it before it rates an overhaul? How about just a tune-up? And we won't even talk about these fenders.

I told my husband my last birthday that I wanted a new birthday suit. This one doesn't fit quite right anymore. It seems to have gotten all stretched out somehow. It could be the five humongous babies I gave birth to. Someone actually tried to help me with a little parent-training program before I had my babies. They said that to prepare for pregnancy I should put on a large, formless dress. Then they said I should stick a beanbag chair down the front—and leave it there for nine months. Then I was told that after nine months, I should take out 10 percent of the beans. It was a helpful exercise in postpartum preparation.

"Bean" There, Done That

Several thousand beans later, this Sister Suzie doesn't have to worry too much about sitting on a thistle. Who could feel it with such a thoroughly bean-padded seat? Even my upper arms look like a couple of giant, overstuffed burritos. It's anything but *bueno*. And believe me, *no one* is whistling—with or without the teeth.

As I wonder where a girl can go for a good de-beaning, I find myself hoping some renowned plastic surgeon will join our church and that he'll feel led to start an extreme makeover ministry for pastors' wives. Sometimes it pays to know someone in the highest makeover places.

Going to Extremes

If you're concerned that I'm on the verge of going to some cosmetic extremes, not to worry. Besides, even the most extreme makeover would be temporary. Nips and tucks aren't the answer. Tucks tend to get untucked. Nips, de-nipped. These bodies are not made to last forever. There's joy when we avoid placing extreme value in temporary things—like looks, for instance, so notorious for their brevity.

It really is all about Who you know. Not cosmetically. Spiritually. As it's been said, "Know Jesus, know joy; no Jesus, no joy." It genuinely pays to know this particular Someone in the highest eternal places.

Holy Frijoles

Honestly, if I'm destined to live out my earthly days as the "Frijole Mama," I'll be okay. Besides, there is a body in my future that is specially designed by my Father to last forever. Philippians 3:20–21 says, "But our citizenship is in heaven. And we eagerly await a Savior from there, the Lord Jesus Christ, who, by the power that enables him to bring everything under his control, will transform our lowly bodies so that they will be like his glorious body."

The funny thing is, I won't have even the slightest concern over how much beanage the new, glorious body has. I'll have fully shifted from an earthly view of things to a holy, heavenly perspective. The heavenly way is the better way.

I'm thankful the Lord doesn't leave us guessing about his better way: "The revelation of GOD is whole and pulls our lives together. The signposts of GOD are clear and point out the right road. The life-maps of GOD are right, showing the way to joy. The directions of GOD are plain and easy on the eyes. GOD's reputation is twenty-four-carat gold, with a lifetime guarantee. The decisions of GOD are accurate down to the nth degree" (Ps. 19:7–9 MSG).

Joy definitely does not come from looking a certain way or from having certain things. Joy comes in knowing, focusing on, and surrendering to Jesus. It comes as we get to know him better through his Word and learn how trustworthy he truly is. And it comes as we find out more about his wonderful plans for our future.

Anytime I ever go extreme, I hope it's always for Jesus—not for any kind of bean-ectomy. A merry, joy-filled Christmas lies in the Jesus extreme. When that's really all I want for Christmas, then I can wish everyone else a merry Christmas in a new way. So Merry Christmas—to all my fellow human beans!

> And a highway will be there;
>   it will be called the Way of Holiness.
> The unclean will not journey on it;
>   it will be for those who walk in that Way;
>   wicked fools will not go about on it.
> No lion will be there,
>   nor will any ferocious beast get up on it;
>   they will not be found there.
> But only the redeemed will walk there,

and the ransomed of the LORD will return.
They will enter Zion with singing;
    everlasting joy will crown their heads.
Gladness and joy will overtake them,
    and sorrow and sighing will flee away.

Isaiah 35:8–10

I'm Living in a Material World   9
Jesus is the fabric of our lives

It's always a big deal to find costumes for the church's Christmas production. Not that there aren't other challenges that go along with a Christmas play. There are tons of big decisions. Do we use real animals again and risk losing another janitor? Do we use a real baby again and rewrite that "no crying he makes" line? When should we really bring in the wise men? And shouldn't we find different wise men than the ones we had last year? They were more like wise guys than wise men. I don't remember reading anywhere in Scripture that the Three Stooges brought gifts from the East. How many "yuck, yucks" does it take to complete a scene, anyway?

But all other production challenges considered, swathing an entire choir and drama group with fabric, convincing the men they are not wearing dresses, and taking care to not end up having anyone looking like a used camel salesman—now that's especially tricky.

Needle Needy

I've found that being a terrible seamstress has actually been a great blessing twice a year: Easter and Christmas. No one ever comes to me for sewing help at either pageant time. All I have to do is tell them about my dress project in Home Ec. I was the only one in class who made two sleeves for the same armhole. Some people are just never meant to be around needles. On the other hand, if the directors come up with a Bible character who has both arms on the same side, I'm their woman. (Did I really use "on the other hand" to begin that sentence?)

I love watching in wonder as the real seamstresses crank out hundreds of costumes and transform your average modern-day church people into a pretty convincing bunch of Bethlehemites. I remember one year, however, we were a little "over-blessed" with a certain teal-colored fabric. One of the costume makers had found a ton of it at an even less-than-bargain-basement price. So I think she bought up the whole basement. Who could resist?

It made some nice costumes, but it looked a little suspicious to have the people of the city, Joseph and Mary, the shepherds, and maybe even a few of the angels all decked out in the same color. How much uni-colored material can one play support? There was such a huge field of teal that there was a rather bluish/greenish tint reflecting off the brass in the orchestra pit, back up to the star, spilling all over the shepherds, the baby Jesus, the manger, the hay—the entire scene. The whole thing had an "under the sea" feeling. I wondered if the Little Mermaid might make a cameo appearance before it was over. Thoughts of seafood during a Christmas play blurs the Christmas focus a little, doesn't it?

Go TEAL It on the Mountain

Whatever color Christmas I'm dreaming of, I hope that—even with a rainbow of distractions—my focus will always come back around to Jesus. Have you ever noticed that the more we shop, the more we tend to want? It's amazing the things we discover we "need" when we're out combing the stores for stuff.

If we're not carefully guarding against loving any of that stuff, our entire Christmas becomes completely off-tint. Loving the right things means not loving things. We can set the Christmas mood for feeding our every weird craving and end up dissatisfied, discontent, and distracted from the real meaning of Christmas. Or we can trade the restlessness that comes from wanting what we don't have for the serenity of having the right focus.

Loving the Lord brings a soul-wealth. It's the kind of wealth that lasts. Loving the things of this world just breeds frustration. Remember what we read in 1 John 2? "Don't love the world's ways. Don't love the world's goods. *Love of the world squeezes out love for the Father.* Practically everything that goes on in the world—wanting your own way, wanting everything for yourself, wanting to appear important—has nothing to do with the Father. It just isolates you from him. The world and all its wanting, wanting, wanting is on the way out—but whoever does what God wants is set for eternity" (vv. 15–17 MSG, emphasis added).

Shop 'Til You Stop

Sometimes we need to stop the shopping, take a little break, and do something more important. It's also amazing what it does for our spirits when we turn off the TV for a while. It's good to take time out from the Christmas ad mania and watch a family video—or even make a new one. Sometimes finding a mission project that the whole family can be involved in is perfect for taking the family focus off of the "things" of Christmas and setting it on the "ministry" of Christmas. Caroling in a retirement home, baking cookies for a lonely neighbor, ministering to the children of those in prison, serving in a soup kitchen for the homeless—so many holiday mission projects, so little holiday! It's an excellent way to make sure Jesus really is the fabric of our lives.

I was thinking we might even try working on some of the projects wearing matching outfits. I hear there's still plenty of teal fabric left over. Just kidding. I think if something like that ever comes up again, I'll just *dye*.

These people think religion is supposed to make you rich. And religion does make your life rich, by making you content with what you have. We didn't bring anything into this world, and we won't take anything with us when we leave. So we should be satisfied just to have food and clothes. People who want to be rich fall into all sorts of temptations and traps. They are caught by foolish and harmful desires that drag them down and destroy them. The love of money causes all kinds of trouble. Some people want money so much that they have given up their faith and caused themselves a lot of pain.

1 Timothy 6:5–10 CEV

Christmas "Spirit"   10
The real Spirit of Christmas? The Holy Spirit!

I just finished another exhausting day of fighting the holiday traffic. The holiday traffic was *inside the store*. I'm not trying to be tacky, but some of those shoppers need to go to traffic school in the worst way. There are mall shoppers who just don't get the unwritten "walk to the right" law and are forever making the mall-ways an unsafe place. The ones who are heavy-laden with bulky bags and never look up are the most dangerous. I had a couple of near miss incidents today. Am I glad I'm insured!

That's still probably not as dangerous as the chemical threat of running into that lady in the department store who won't let you pass until she's sufficiently doused you with perfume. You try to slip by without making eye contact, but she chases you down. That's when fight or flight kicks in and you have to decide if you're going to take the chemical spritz like a mature adult, or if the little squirt-happy lady dressed in black is going down. Ahh, the air is filled with Christmas spirit.

Clearing the Air

While I'm clearing the air, how about the person who gets into a "20 items or less" checkout line with enough loot to open his own franchise? That's a shopper who is altogether overdue for a refresher course in consumer etiquette. Then there are the aisle hoggers. They park their carts in the middle and block cart traffic north, south, east, and west bound. Sometimes they hold little mini-reunions with long-lost friends, oblivious to the multi-cart pileups around them. Why is it that what I need is always right behind the reunion? It's even worse when, instead of a face-to-face reunion, the person is having an all-consuming cell phone dialogue. Everyone else either waits (sort of like vicarious call waiting) or tries to maneuver around the already over-packed aisle (a very dangerous maneuver that should only be attempted by professionals).

I saw something that may have topped them all the other day though. It was free sample day, and I spotted a consumer who had done a bit too much consuming. If there's anything more thrilling than free samples, it's free samples in the candy department. Just as my mouth started to water, I spotted this gal who was obviously operating a cart under the influence of fudge! Her cart was totally out of control. She had full cheeks, a giant brown splotch on one cheek, and a little fudgy hunk in one hand. It was one of the most hilarious and disturbing shopping sights I've seen. I had a really good snicker to myself. You gotta love a girl who is into fudge to the exclusion of all safety concerns. Despite the cart danger, I decided against making a citizen's arrest. I hope there were no injuries.

Under What Influence?

Of course, it's sad to mention what has some Christmas shoppers under the influence. So many people's idea of "spirits" at Christmas is definitely the wrong kind of Christmas "spirit." I don't care what they say; the symbol of Christmas is not a bottle. Why would anyone want to have a Christmas they can't remember? It's the kind of Christmas "celebrating" that literally destroys lives. Injuries occur—on so many levels.

When people celebrate through a bottle, they're out of control. They lose their inhibitions, and the booze is what controls them. It's a chemical dousing of the saddest kind. As those who've given our lives to the Savior, the Bible reminds us not to give away control to spirits but to be controlled by the Holy Spirit. "Therefore do not be foolish, but understand what the Lord's will is. Do not get drunk on wine, which leads to debauchery. Instead, be filled with the Spirit" (Eph. 5:17–18).

More Filling

His holy influence in the very deepest part of who you are can make a night-and-day difference in the way you see yourself, the way you see others, and the way you respond in every happenstance of life. Being filled with the Spirit of Christ fills your life with meaning.

Ask the Holy Spirit to fill you, to take control of every part of your life, your every breath, your every Christmas minute. He can even make a shopping trip with the worst etiquette school dropouts seem like a walk in the candy shop.

So I say, live by the Spirit, and you will not gratify the desires of the sinful nature. For the sinful nature desires what is contrary to the Spirit, and the Spirit what is contrary to the sinful nature. They are in conflict with each other, so that you do not do what you want. But if you are led by the Spirit, you are not under law. The acts of the sinful nature are obvious: sexual immorality, impurity and debauchery; idolatry and witchcraft; hatred, discord, jealousy, fits of rage, selfish ambition, dissensions, factions and envy; drunkenness, orgies, and the like. I warn you, as I did before, that those who live like this will not inherit the kingdom of God.

But the fruit of the Spirit is love, joy, peace, patience, kindness, goodness, faithfulness, gentleness and self-control. Against such things there is no law. Those who belong to Christ Jesus have crucified the sinful nature with its passions and desires. Since we live by the Spirit, let us keep in step with the Spirit.

Galatians 5:16–25

Part 3

Hearts Will Be Glowing When Loved Ones Draw Near

Clinging to the Family Plan

Right to Assemble   11
Assembling the family for a happy holiday

C hristmas requires major preps. Not just the lists, the buying, the wrapping, and the party planning. But the time of year requires some special preparatory training. I've been working on a special training program of my own. I think, for instance, if I started in August I could get my trainees ready by December.

In phase one of the program, the trainees would learn to carry four times their body weight in bags and packages while carrying six rolls of wrapping paper, a soft drink, and a pretzel. Then, while still balancing the packages, paper, drink, and pretzel, each trainee would be required to find the car, dig out the keys, and open the trunk. All this would be done, of course, while trying to corral a toddler who needs to go potty.

Physically Unfit in the Twinkie of an Eye

You would think that kind of Christmas aerobic routine would keep a trainee slim and trim, wouldn't you? But I'm afraid that brings us to phase two of the training, which would include an intensive overeating regimen. The diet would be made up of approximately 60 percent fast food and 60 percent sugar. That extra 20 percent could be applied directly to the pudgy middle—sort of like a dessert with a creamy filling. This is the season so many of us become more Twinkie-like than ever before. On the special training diet, program participants would be guaranteed to have their stomachs sufficiently stretched out by Thanksgiving, when the real Christmas overeating season begins.

Easy Assembly

We do put a lot into preparing for Christmas. We list, we cook, we decorate, we buy, we assemble. Ah, the assembling. A big part of preparing for Christmas morning involves putting together a train set, a dollhouse, a bike, or some other large piece of machinery with more moving parts than a *Star Wars* speeder. All the riding toys are especially known for their concentrated ulcer potential. Parents should be warned before putting together any riding toy that "easy assembly" actually means "easy assembly if you have a doctorate in engineering and are fluent in twelve languages."

I remember one Christmas Richie and I were doing one of those "easy assemblies" on a bike. I wondered how the manufacturer was able to fit an entire bike into such a tiny box. I understood—in an overwhelmingly frightening sort of way—when we opened the box and I saw the thing was in about 47,000 pieces.

Then I hauled a huge book out of the bottom of the box. "Oh, look. How thoughtful; they gave us a free St. Louis phone book."

"That's the instruction booklet," he said. If that thing was a "booklet," then my thirty-pound Christmas ham was a "hamlet." I kept searching in the box, hoping I'd find a condensed version—or at least maybe some CliffsNotes. Sorry, I don't think there's any sufficient way to prepare for that part of Christmas.

Preps or no preps, the bike went together—even rolled in the right direction. The bike and the entire Christmas were a huge hit. We even had bike parts left over. I worried for several years that might come back to haunt us. No lawsuits to date.

To be honest, it wasn't really the bike that made Christmas such a success. It was a different kind of "assembly." We determined to make time for some "family assembly."

Christmas—Some Assembly Required

Gathering together as families is a wonderful part of Christmas. We can get so caught up in the urgency of Christmas busyness that we miss the real urgency of time spent with family, the urgency of sharing the Savior's birth with our children. When our children are young, it's vital that we teach them what a real Christmas celebration is all about. As they grow older—even after they're grown and gone—we still provide an example to them of celebrating in the right way.

Even in the busiest part of the season when assembling isn't particularly easy, we'll find that making family memories will give us something distinctively extraordinary to tuck away and treasure, just as Mary did in Luke 2:51 when she "treasured up all these things and pondered them in her heart."

Let's include plenty of the right kind of assembly in our Christmas season. We can assemble meaning, joy, and peace into a Christmas that's centered on the love of our Savior.

The Bible tells us that the shepherds assembled at that first Christmas. The angels assembled too. Even great, wise men assembled a little later. Assembling in the name of the Christ of Christmas is a magnificently rewarding assembly. It is right to assemble! And unlike bikes, speeders, and other wheeled vehicles, you hardly ever have parts left over.

Suddenly a great company of the heavenly host appeared with the angel, praising God and saying, "Glory to God in the highest, and on earth peace to men on whom his favor rests." When the angels had left them and gone into heaven, the shepherds said to one another, "Let's go to Bethlehem and see this thing that has happened, which the Lord has told us about." So they hurried off and found Mary and Joseph, and the baby, who was lying in the manger. When they had seen him, they spread the word concerning what had been told them about this child, and all who heard it were amazed at what the shepherds said to them. But Mary treasured up all these things and pondered them in her heart.

Luke 2:13–19

Forgiveness Is Relative   12
To err is human, to forgive can keep you out of jail

I was chatting with a friend who was fretting over all the stress at Christmas. I said something like, "At least we'll have those big family get-togethers." She replied that *that's* what she was fretting about. She popped a couple of Tums as she told me about her uncle.

"Over the river and through the woods, to Uncle Bob's house? Oh no!" It seems her uncle Bob makes every family gathering an extremely strenuous exercise in keeping her cool. She said she has to fight rather felonious thoughts related to good ol' Uncle Bob. *How bad would it really be to set fire to his barn?* But who wants a Christmas family get-together that ends with a jail sentence?

We all tend to have at least one Uncle Bob–type relative who could use a remedial people-skills class or two and who seems to be, shall we say, a few nuts over the fruitcake maximum. He's known for telling bad jokes and keeping his turkey-eating teeth in his wife's purse. He laughs hysterically as he tells the family (yet again) every stupid thing you ever did growing up. You know going in to the family party that there will be noogies and wedgies with your name on them—even though you're over thirty. And whatever you do, never, NEVER pull his finger.

This Means War

Some of us have challenging relatives who aren't just annoying. They're on the offensive—planning the Christmas attack. They might use the guilt weapon, or maybe they harshly disapprove of whatever we're excited about at the moment. Maybe it's a problem with explosive anger. Some are real rascals who seem bent on offending. What's a nonviolent, non-noogie-lover to do?

The annoyances? We can rise above those in the power of Christ. The real grievances? We're called to forgive those. Colossians 3:13 says, "You must make allowance for each other's faults and forgive the person who offends you. Remember, the Lord forgave you, so you must forgive others" (NLT).

When we forgive the way the Lord forgives us, the battle is essentially over. Forgiveness is actually quite stress relieving. Does it make the family member behave any better? Sorry, no. As a matter of fact, it doesn't really change the offender at all. But it does change the forgiver.

Constrained to Forgive

Jesus told a story about the requirement of forgiveness. A king showed mercy on a man who owed him something like a gazillion dollars—more than he could repay in a lifetime. Then the man turned right around and went ballistic over a debt of a few bucks. He refused to forgive the piddly debt. The passage tells us that the king was so angry about the guy refusing to forgive when he had been forgiven so much, that he tossed the guy into prison and essentially threw away the key.

Our sin debt was bigger than we could ever pay. Jesus came as a baby; lived a perfect, sinless life; then died a horrifying death on the cross. The Son of God on a cross — there's no higher payment. And he forgives our debt willingly. How can we not forgive another person's offense when we've been forgiven every horrible thing we've ever done?

Forgiving doesn't mean that we're saying what the person did was okay. It means we're choosing not to hold it against him. We're choosing not to become bitter. Bitterness is the destroyer of Christmas celebrations. It destroys joy.

Have you ever sensed that your happiness was just beyond your reach, but you couldn't quite put your finger on why? (No, not the Uncle Bob kind of finger.) All you know is that even fudge doesn't taste quite as good. Bitterness puts a dark cloud over even the nicest gift, and it can unexpectedly explode out of our lives in all kinds of surprising directions.

Forgiveness is essential for keeping our relationship right with the Lord. Matthew 6:14–15 says, "In prayer there is a connection between what God does and what you do. You can't get forgiveness from God, for instance, without also forgiving others. If you refuse to do your part, you cut yourself off from God's part" (MSG).

We grieve our Father when we hang on to unforgiveness. He knows our unforgiveness grows into bitterness and ugly anger that lashes out. Ephesians 4:30–32 tells us, "And do not grieve the Holy Spirit of God, with whom you were sealed for the day of redemption. Get rid of all bitterness, rage and anger, brawling and slander, along with every form of malice. Be kind and compassionate to one another, forgiving each other, just as in Christ God forgave you."

Choose Forgiveness

Is there a negative mother-in-law who seems determined to slice and dice you at every gathering? How about a nitpicking sister who seems almost bent on offending? Forgive her and decide not to let her ruin Jesus's birthday celebration for you. Bitterness is a prison we inflict on ourselves. We can send ourselves to bitterness jail without setting our own uncle Bob's barn on fire. But when we forgive, we free ourselves from that prison. Then when there's a need to confront, we can confront in love and mercy, with reconciliation as the goal.

Staying in touch with a good, positive, supportive friend who can steer us toward Scripture helps. If you're struggling with a difficult family member, remind yourself a few extra times that, while that person may not appreciate you, God loves you dearly. Focus on God's Christmas love more than the other person's hatefulness. Stay on guard for bitterness and you'll be guarding your Christmas joy.

You might want to stay on guard in other ways too. A "wedgie watch" couldn't hurt.

> Then Peter came to Jesus and asked, "Lord, how many times shall I forgive my brother when he sins against me? Up to seven times?"
>
> Jesus answered, "I tell you, not seven times, but seventy-seven times." . . .
>
> "Then the master called the servant in. 'You wicked servant,' he said, 'I canceled all that debt of yours because you begged me to. Shouldn't you have had mercy on your fellow servant just as I had on you?' In anger his master turned him over to the jailers to be tortured, until he should pay back all he owed.
>
> "This is how my heavenly Father will treat each of you unless you forgive your brother from your heart."
>
> Matthew 18:21–22, 32–35

Little Drummer Dude   13
Giving our families what they really need? Priceless.

omen tend to love the thrill of the hunt when it comes to
shopping. My husband is a pounce-and-conquer, kill-and-
go-home kind of guy. He dashes into the store, grabs the
item he's looking for (or something "close enough"), pays whatever
is on the tag, and dashes back home. Me? Picture me in full hunting
garb stealthily tracking down the beast of a bargain, carefully taking
aim, then deciding I should probably look at all the other beasts before
I shoot—just to make sure I'm getting the best one. I've been known
to spend an extra ten dollars in gas driving over a county line or two
while on safari—all to save a buck fifty.

It's all about the thrill of the bargain hunt. It's delightfully gratifying
to a woman to get a compliment on a new pair of cute shoes and to be
able to answer, "I got them for $4.99 from the going-out-of-business/
discount/clearance/liquidation rack at the below-wholesale store!"

Is there anything more exhilarating than finally hitting on that ideal
gift at a bargain price? It's downright inspirational when you can get
the perfect gift for a song!

Giving Jesus a Song?

I've always loved singing "The Little Drummer Boy" at Christmas.
It seems even more touching now that I'm an adult (and now that I
do most of the shopping) and I realize what it meant to get the perfect
gift for a song. Literally, a song.

I wonder what my kids would do if I told them it was time to open presents, and then I got out the guitar and sang a number or two. "Merry Christmas, kids!" Can you picture their little mouths hanging open? Their wide-eyed stares? *"You're giving us a song for Christmas?"* I have a feeling the gift would leave a lot to be desired. More accurately, a truckload to be desired. Even before considering the fact that I only know about three and a half chords on the guitar.

But do you know what's special to me about that little drummer boy? There's such a sweet story at the heart of that song. All the boy wanted was to give something to Jesus. And all he had to give was a song. What a sweet encouragement it is to us when we think about a boy giving the only thing he could think to give (not very valuable in the world's eyes) and then—oh, glorious thought—Jesus smiled at the gift and the giver.

Marching to the Beat of a Different Drummer

A merry Christmas sometimes means going against the norm. Conventional wisdom tells us that hunting down the right gifts will lead to a merry Christmas. But meeting our family's real needs at Christmas is not about our presents. It's more about our presence. We need to be there for each other. We have to guard our family time to make sure we're really providing physically, emotionally, and spiritually. Nothing beats our attention. Pa rum pa pum pum.

First Timothy 3 says, "If anyone wants to provide leadership in the church, good! . . . He must handle his own affairs well, attentive to his own children and having their respect. For if someone is unable to handle his own affairs, how can he take care of God's church?" (vv. 1, 4–5 MSG). We're providing for our family when we're "attentive" to them.

Women are given a specific charge a few verses later: "No exceptions are to be made for women—same qualifications: serious, dependable, not sharp-tongued, not overfond of wine. Servants in the church are to be committed to their spouses, attentive to their own children, and diligent in looking after their own affairs. Those who do this servant work will come to be highly respected, a real credit to this Jesus-faith" (vv. 11–13 MSG).

Keeping Time

Since I truly want to be a real credit to this Jesus-faith, I'm working to keep up with my time better. Keeping time is more than just staying on the beat. It's guarding special family dates on the calendar. It's focusing on more than just getting the right gifts. Planning memory-making times, doing the decorating, shopping and partying together, and creating plenty of family ministry projects can have a big part in giving our family the right kind of attention. Can you imagine Jesus smiling?

We can stay tuned in to giving our family the best kind of attention when we make sure we've first given everything we have to the Lord—time, talents, money—all. Giving our all to Jesus is the very best gift we can give to our families. It's giving our children a parent who is in sync with the God of the universe. It's a genuinely priceless gift that we can pass from generation to generation.

And the beat goes on.

Charge [the people] thus, so that they may be without reproach and blameless. If anyone fails to provide for his relatives, and especially for those of his own family, he has disowned the faith [by failing to accompany it with fruits] and is worse than an unbeliever [who performs his obligation in these matters].

1 Timothy 5:7–8 AMP

Christmas Is Like a Box of Chocolates

14

What do we find in its chewy center?

Cream-filled or gooey center? That is the question. The journey to the center of a chocolate is a sweet adventure. Coconut or caramel? Nougat or nut? Mint or mocha? The possibilities are enough to make a chocolate enthusiast plumb giddy. Anticipation of the surprise inside could tingle any chocolate-loving spine. It's the reason we can pinch an entire box of chocolates and get the inside story on each one in two minutes flat—under the two-minute mark if we're in a "pinch." There's a ravenous hunger to know what's in the center—usually followed closely by a ravenous hunger to eat it.

Every once in a while, though, the pinch is the source of some major choco-disenchantment. There's a certain brownish jelly-type goo that causes my nose to squinch in a look of disgust and disappointment. What is that stuff? And what's it doing in the middle of my chocolate?

I've heard there are worse things to find in your chocolates. Just in case you'd ever like to research some of them, here are my top ten (barring the ones that were just too disgusting to mention):

Top Ten Things You Never Want to Find in the Center of Your Christmas Chocolates

10. Microfilm with schematics for the new Mach 937 stealth fighter
 9. Magma

8. A fortune that reads "A distant relative will come for a lengthy visit"

7. Another chocolate, with another chocolate inside of that, and another chocolate inside of that, and another . . .

6. A slip of paper that starts with the words, "Your weight is . . ."

5. A clown that pops out to the tune of "Pop Goes the Weasel"

4. A warning label that reads "Not to be taken internally"

3. Legs of any kind, size, or shape

2. One of the evil Penguin's dehydrated henchmen (but if you find one, Batman will know what to do)

1. An expiration date—especially if it refers to any time now considered "retro"

Just as we don't want to find anything in the center of our chocolates that doesn't belong, we want to make sure we don't find anything at the center of our Christmas that doesn't belong.

It's easy for our kids to let the man in red take center stage at Christmas. That jolly old elf is on the minds of most kids from the jingle of the first bell of the season—especially since most of them believe he sees them when they're sleeping, and knows when they're awake. In reality, that thought is a little creepy to me. Who is this guy who eats all the Christmas cookies and drinks a billion or two glasses of milk every Christmas Eve?

Is Santa really coming to town? Santa Claus, St. Nicholas, Kriss Kringle, Father Christmas, Sinterklaas, Father Frost, Père Noël—talk about a lot of aliases! And if you ask what a family should do with Santa, you're likely to get answers that vary from here to the North Pole.

Christmas Confession

Brace yourself. I'm about to reveal some extremely personal, enormously juicy information here. (I feel like my cream center is showing.) My husband and I chose to tell our kids the truth about Santa from the get-go. We told them they could pretend if they wanted to. But we wanted to make sure they would never doubt that anything we told them was true. We have five kids. We figured if even one might struggle with the reality of Santa versus the reality of Jesus, it just wasn't worth the risk.

Some say our kids were a little gypped, missing some of the magical wonder and fantasy of Christmas. Four out of the five of them are teens now (I hope this leads you to pray for me regularly), so I asked them how they felt about that. They shrugged and told me they were "fine." Teenagers.

Let me rush to say that lots of parents choose to play Santa and are perfectly delighted with the fun and games. It's a parent call. But no matter how we choose to treat the Santa issue, one thing is for sure. Our children need to be reminded that Christmas is not all about the guy in the red suit who brings gifts once a year. Christmas is about the Savior of the world, Jesus Christ. He is the unmatched, unequalled gift of Christmas.

Yes, Virginia, There Really Is a Jesus

Here's a radical concept: Christmas doesn't have to be Santa-centered. Or gift-centered. Or even others-centered. The very heart of Christmas should always be Christ. And we can choose to make it that way, to center on the real and living One who brought us salvation. Luke 1:69 says, "He set the power of salvation in the center of our lives" (MSG). It's a no-surprises center that gives us power for living in his love.

Focusing in on his love will keep our families truly centered. Jude 20–21 says, "But you, dear friends, carefully build yourselves up in this most holy faith by praying in the Holy Spirit, staying right at the center of God's love, keeping your arms open and outstretched, ready for the mercy of our Master, Jesus Christ. This is the unending life, the real

life!" (MSG). Living in his love gives us that real and unending life
that no one can take away—not even one of Penguin's henchmen!

> Blessed be the Lord, the God of Israel;
>   he came and set his people free.
> He set the power of salvation in the center of our lives,
>   and in the very house of David his servant,
> Just as he promised long ago
>   through the preaching of his holy prophets:
> Deliverance from our enemies
>   and every hateful hand;
> Mercy to our fathers,
>   as he remembers to do what he said he'd do,
> What he swore to our father Abraham—
>   a clean rescue from the enemy camp,
> So we can worship him without a care in the world,
>   made holy before him as long as we live.
>
>   Luke 1:68–75 MSG

Frosty the Snow-Lonely Man   15
Understanding our need for each other

I would have to be pretty desperate for a friend to try to build one
for myself. And at the remote chance I did decide to construct
myself an imaginary-type friend, I think I would make it out of
something a lot more huggable than snow. Brrr.

One thing is sure: if I ever happened to put a hat on a big hunk
of snow and it started to dance around, the next words spoken would
likely be "Hand me the paddles! Clear!"

Growing up in Texas, my family considered snow too valuable to use it to build imaginary friends. No, we used it to pelt each other. I can hardly remember anything quite as sweet as seeing a friend's bangs fly to the back of her head as a giant snowball would explode right smack-dab on the forehead target. I wish I had some of those on tape. I would love to be able to say, "Let's see that again in slow motion." Back then I would invariably rub it in with something corny like, "It's been nice snowin' ya!" Now those are some sweet Christmas memories.

Memories May Be Beautiful, and Yet . . .

Memories can be oh so sweet. But some of them can also be haunting. Everyone suffers loss at one time or another. Christmas is the season of family and friends gathering—and the season we picture everything in our lives in harmony and perfect order. Sometimes that reminds us in a new way of loved ones we've lost, pain we've suffered, even failures and disappointments we've experienced. There probably aren't many people who don't have their own ghosts of Christmas past.

They say time heals all wounds, but that's not always true. Sometimes depression has physical origins beyond our control. Then again, sometimes we choose to hang on to pain, to focus and dwell on what hurts the most until it becomes all consuming. It's all we can see. That pain we're dwelling on becomes bigger and more real to us than the bigness of God. We should never ignore the hurt, but if we choose to focus on it to the exclusion of God's work in our lives—his love and grace and power to heal—then we're dragged into bigger pain, hopelessness, and depression. We can get to the place where we're afraid to move on. The pain is what we know. It becomes familiar—it even becomes our life. And if it's a failure we're dealing with, sometimes we let the constant fear of failing again cripple us.

Defrosting

Our heavenly Father doesn't want us to be frozen by the ghosts of Christmas past. He has something so much better for us than a life of depression. The kind of depression that's caused by focusing on pain will chip away our hope. Putting pain in perspective and past failures behind us brings new hope.

In Philippians 3:13, Paul says, "No, dear brothers and sisters, I am still not all I should be, but I am focusing all my energies on this one thing: Forgetting the past and looking forward to what lies ahead" (NLT). Eyes off the past, eyes on the future.

We can have living hope because of our living Savior. "Praise be to the God and Father of our Lord Jesus Christ! In his great mercy he has given us new birth into a living hope through the resurrection of Jesus Christ from the dead" (1 Peter 1:3).

Like Scrooge awoke to a new world, you can too. God's mercies are new every morning. Make a new start. Trade the focus on pain for promises from his Word that you have a hope and future. Trade guilt over failures for the forgiveness he offers through his great mercies. God has a plan for your Christmas—and your life. "'For I know the plans I have for you,' declares the LORD, 'plans to prosper you and not to harm you, plans to give you hope and a future'" (Jer. 29:11).

Warm Up to the Family

If you've been tempted to isolate yourself ("crawl in a hole," as one of my friends describes it), fight that temptation all the way to victory. God designed you, and he built into you a need for people. There's warmth in the family. Whether it's your birth family or your re-birth family—your church—it can help melt away some of that chilly feeling you're experiencing. Don't worry, it's a good melting.

If your family is around and you've been pushing them away, stop giving them the cold shoulder. Come back. If you've let church slide, come back to your church family. Hebrews 10:25 says, "And let us not neglect our meeting together, as some people do, but encourage and warn each other, especially now that the day of his coming back again is drawing near" (NLT). Even Frosty said, "I'll be back again someday." But we're instructed to be together, so don't wait for someday.

Stressing Friendships

Does that mean that dealing with people will always be a walk in the park? Hardly. It can be a big-time stress factor. But a necessary one. And believe it or not, stress isn't always a bad thing.

Stress can actually be a good force working in our lives to help us focus. It's stress that helps a person survive in times of danger. It can help us rally to meet a challenge. There is no life on this planet that is completely free from stress—nor should there be. But if we handle stressful situations in positive ways and respond appropriately, our bodies are designed to give us a sweet feeling of relaxation.

Stress becomes a problem when the body skips that relaxation part and stays stuck in the tension. That's when physical and emotional problems can crop up. Likewise, isolating ourselves can also create physical and emotional problems. Making room for people in our lives, while it can cause stress, can be a stress reliever too.

Through it all, we need to keep focusing on the goodness of God and the blessings he's provided. There's gracious blessing and refreshment there—straight from the Father.

And when it comes to graciousness, there's snow-body better!

Be devoted to one another in brotherly love. Honor one another above yourselves. Never be lacking in zeal, but keep your spiritual fervor, serving the Lord. Be joyful in hope, patient in affliction, faithful in prayer. Share with God's people who are in need. Practice hospitality.

Bless those who persecute you; bless and do not curse. Rejoice with those who rejoice; mourn with those who mourn. Live in harmony with one another. Do not be proud, but be willing to associate with people of low position. Do not be conceited.

Romans 12:10–16

Part 4

Have Yourself a Merry Little Christmas

Keeping Our Christmas Joy

Jumping for Joy to the World 16
Holiday blues vs. joy in Jesus

We have some friends who bought their kids a trampoline for Christmas. Everything was great until Christmas Eve when they were trying to put the thing together. It was bad enough that they had to wrestle with it in the freezing garage, but she would stretch one way and it would pull out his side. He would tug the other way and mess up her side.

The military husband told his wife to pretend she knew how to make an army bunk. That only made her mad, and the whole thing became a giant tug-of-war. Pretty soon it wasn't even about putting the stinkin' trampoline together. It was about winning. They were both so determined to win that they stretched that trampoline top onto a frame that they found out later didn't really fit! This couple now has biceps like nobody's business. And I think their trampoline is so tight that if the kids can ever get a good enough bounce, the thing is surely strong enough to shoot them clean over to the Stop-n-Go around the corner.

I laughed when they were telling me about it, but actually it reminded me all too well of trying to squirm into my black pants. They fit perfectly in October. But by the end of December, I was stretching this way, tugging that way. Military corners are fine for bunks, but who wants a pair of pants you can bounce a quarter off? Now that's depressing.

Bounce This Around

Statistics tell us that more people become depressed around Christmas than any other time of year. The stresses of the busy season can stretch us tighter than the tightest trampoline. High expectations that are tough to meet can leave people disappointed. Holiday memories can remind us of loved ones we deeply miss.

Sadness isn't always a bad thing. It's a way of dealing with difficulties. It's when we get stuck in the sadness that we have a serious problem. That's when it's time to go on an earnest joy hunt.

We need to be as determined to win the battle of the blues as my friends were to win the battle of the tramp. Like them, we can build muscle in the strain if we don't quit. Romans 12:11–12 says, "Be alert servants of the Master, cheerfully expectant. Don't quit in hard times; pray all the harder" (MSG).

Is it really possible to stay "cheerfully expectant"? That's the kind of Christmas cheer our heavenly Father wants us to have!

Let's look at a few practical things we can do—or encourage a friend to do—when battling the blues.

Ten Ways to Help Beat the Holiday Blues

1. **See your doctor.** If depression has been nagging at you for a while, or even if it's just snapping at your heels, check in with your doctor. There may be other physical factors at work, and your physician has ways to rule out some internal and external depression instigators and can offer some great helps for relief.

2. **Eat more than just fudge.** I know you're thinking I've tiptoed over the hypocritical line, but I can't argue with the fact that a balanced diet helps reduce bad stress and can help alleviate depression. Vitamin, mineral, and herb supplements may also help (but always run these by your doctor first). Since what

we eat affects our mood, eating sensibly can be like ingesting joy.

3. **Guard your quiet time with the Lord.** When there is a joy need, God's Word is our prescription. Try a good dose of Philippians (take two chapters and call me in the morning). Philippians is a book of tremendous joy. It's not circumstance-based joy. Paul was in prison when he wrote it. It's Jesus-based joy—and that's the lasting kind. Dwell on the promises of God. Remember his faithfulness.

4. **Guard your rest time.** Don't overwhelm yourself with activity. Find a reasonable balance in the schedule. Remember that cutting out some of the activity is not necessarily a bad thing. Don't feel guilty; no one can do it all. Since unmerited guilt is another depression inducer, save guilt for the real sins in your life. It's not selfish for you to take a little time for yourself and do something you enjoy that can help you gain some perspective.

5. **Guard your friend time.** While you shouldn't overwhelm yourself with activity, we already mentioned that isolating yourself isn't the right move either. If some holiday blues are threatening, remember that you have a God-given need for people.

6. **Work on meeting someone else's needs for a while.** Focusing on the needs of others is not only a ministry and a service, but it's also great for giving us a renewed perspective of what we have. It can give us a little math-type help in counting our own blessings and helps us stop focusing on only the negatives in our lives.

7. **Watch out for worry.** Do what you can to nix unnecessary stress. Fretting over those extra calories from yesterday's party and that check you wrote last Friday isn't going to help. Do what you can to alleviate the problems, but don't let worry increase your stress level needlessly.

8. **Exercise.** Health experts agree that there is great stress-reducing value in exercise. Some doctors suggest that exercise three times

a week or more is as valuable as any antidepressant meds they could prescribe. Check in with your doctor first, but if you have to take some of the other activities off your schedule to plug in some exercise, you'll likely get more accomplished in the end—and you'll have more fun doing it. Exercise increases your energy level and generates chemicals in the brain that fight depression. If you can get a little exercise outdoors, that's even better. Sunshine doesn't always come easy in the winter months, but it can help ward off depression too. If the weather cooperates, a walk outside might be just the ticket.

9. **Check your expectations at the door.** Expecting events to go exactly as you've envisioned or expecting people to respond just how you've imagined is a ticket to Disappointment-ville. You can't control every aspect of an event, and you can't control any aspect of a person. Don't try to change someone else's behavior. Work more on your responses. If you anticipate a few snags along the way, you won't be thrown for a loop when they happen. Disappointment because we haven't built "the perfect Christmas" can lead to holiday blues. Find joy even when your plans haven't panned out exactly as expected.

10. **Stay focused on Jesus—it's the most important thing.** It's the answer to every life question and every difficulty. Ask him to give you genuine Christmas cheer that starts right down in your soul. He knows your heart, and only he knows how to fix it when it's breaking. He can make a sad heart sing again. Psalm 9:2 says, "I will be filled with joy because of you. I will sing praises to your name, O Most High" (NLT).

When we stick with Christ, he can give us that bona fide Christmas cheer. So go ahead. Bounce back from the blues. No trampoline required.

Now I'm jumping for joy,
    and shouting and singing my thanks to him.
GOD is all strength for his people,
    ample refuge for his chosen leader;
Save your people
    and bless your heritage.
Care for them;
    carry them like a good shepherd.

                                    Psalm 28:7–9 MSG

Blue Christmas   17
You better not pout, I'm telling you why

Why is it I become a total candle maniac at Christmastime more than any other time of the year? My family thinks I'm a few inches short of a full length of wick. I've wondered if I might like all the candles for warmth's sake. I spend most of my Christmas rather blue—but it's not the "being glum" blue. It's a total lack of blood flow. I think I'm developing some arterial ice crystals. When the weather outside is frightful, a few dozen candles can be so delightful.

Maybe it's more than just a temperature thing, though. I love the electrical twinkly lights of Christmas too—and they're not known for putting out a lot of heat. Granted, they can be frustrating like nothing else. I test the lights before they go on the tree, but by the time I've woven them through a gajillion prickly branches and plugged them in, none of them work. Why is it that one bad bulb spoils the whole strand? Don't the twinkly light manufacturers know the "one bad apple" expression? Ninety-nine working bulbs, and one little non-twinkler can put out the whole strand. I've also wondered why, when you do find the bad bulb, it's usually only after checking the entire other ninety-nine. At least I get a spiritual lesson out of it. I feel like a shepherdess leaving the ninety and nine to search for the one. It's a lot of trouble, but I just have to have the twinkles.

Star Quality

Maybe it's not the warmth or just the sparkle quality that draws me to the little lights every year. I do love thinking about the first real twinkle of Christmas—it was from a star.

Matthew tells us about the wise men from the east who knew to watch for this particular twinkle. "The star appeared to them, guiding them to Bethlehem. It went ahead of them and stopped over the place where the child was. When they saw the star, they were filled with joy! They entered the house where the child and his mother, Mary, were, and they fell down before him and worshiped him. Then they opened their treasure chests and gave him gifts of gold, frankincense, and myrrh" (Matt. 2:9–11 NLT). How's that for directional lights? The wise men had their own "On Star."

True Christmas Light

We need to be wise and follow the light—just as the wise men followed the star right to Jesus. Our light isn't a candle or a strand of twinkles. It's not even a star. No, it's Jesus Christ, the Savior! Isaiah 9:2 prophesied the coming Messiah, letting us know even before his arrival that Jesus would be the real light of Christmas: "The people who walked in darkness have seen a great light. For those who lived in a land of deep shadows—light! sunbursts of light!" (MSG).

Jesus is the light of Christmas—and the Light of the whole world. He said in John 8:12, "I am the light of the world. Whoever follows me will never walk in darkness, but will have the light of life."

Following Jesus means coming out of darkness and walking in the path he illuminates for us. Not understanding the real light or the purpose for the holiday will snuff out joy. Sadly, every person with a purposeless Christmas is a person who's destined for an empty, blue Christmas. The passage in Isaiah 9 that prophesies Christ's coming begins with these words: "Nevertheless, there will be no more gloom for those who were in distress" (v. 1). Follow the light of Christ and you'll be led straight to lasting joy.

So You Better Not Pout

There are plenty of good reasons not to pout. I'm telling you why. Pouting makes wrinkles. Who needs more of those? When you're pouting you can't enjoy the twinkle of tree lights and candles. If you only need two reasons not to pout, how about these: wrinkles and twinkles. But the best reason of all is that Jesus is the light that chases darkness right out of our hearts. Second Corinthians 4:6 says, "For God, who said, 'Let light shine out of darkness,' made his light shine in our hearts to give us the light of the knowledge of the glory of God in the face of Christ."

How excellent it is to have the warmth of his twinkle right here in our hearts. It's also oh-so-excellent to know that the bulbs never go out!

> The people walking in darkness
>   have seen a great light;
> on those living in the land of the shadow of death
>   a light has dawned. . . .
> For to us a child is born,
>   to us a son is given,
>   and the government will be on his shoulders.

And he will be called
> Wonderful Counselor, Mighty God,
> Everlasting Father, Prince of Peace.
Of the increase of his government and peace
> there will be no end.
He will reign on David's throne
> and over his kingdom,
establishing and upholding it
> with justice and righteousness
> from that time on and forever.
The zeal of the LORD Almighty
> will accomplish this.

Isaiah 9:2, 6–7

Prepare Him Room   18

*Making room for Jesus
is making room for joy*

What excuse could the innkeepers have possibly come up with that first Christmas that would have been good enough to justify allowing the Son of God to be born in a barn? Sure, they had that census crowd excuse going for them. But how many hugely pregnant ladies do you imagine rode in on donkeys that week? Didn't anyone there think of saying, "You know what? I'm not giving birth tonight. Take my room and I'll bunk with the cows instead"?

In all fairness, maybe they really were overwhelmed because of their Census Week Special. I can envision an ad slogan something like, "You count 'em up, we'll put 'em up." Hey, it's better than "We may not have HBO, but at least there are no lice." Maybe they had a big "kids stay free" campaign, though I'm guessing they would have to specify on their promotional fliers that young livestock were not included. I wonder if that would bring enough business to light up their "no vacancy" sign.

Or maybe they lost some rooms. Maybe they were recovering from a big Pharisee convention (I hear they were notorious for making off with all the towels). It could've been a pool problem that shut them down. Or maybe the Bethlehem City Inspector wouldn't give the okay for occupancy for all the rooms until they updated their sprinkler system. Surely they had a good reason to be so full they couldn't spare a single room.

No Room

I had my own "no room" situation recently—on a smaller, domestic scale. I was getting ready for a Christmas party, but there was absolutely no room to spare in the fridge for the party food. Someone was definitely going to have to make the room. It was frightening to know it had to be me.

It always makes me nervous when it's time to clean the refrigerator, and I open the door, and I hear *voices*. Now I know what you're thinking. You're not at all surprised that I hear voices and you wonder how long I've been off the medication. But that's not it. The voices are not the usual ones coming from my head. No, these are voices coming from the various plastic containers. I hate it when I walk toward the garbage disposal with one of the containers, open it up, and hear it scream, "I want to LIVE!"

LIVING to the Fullest

While I don't necessarily love listening to my leftovers, I admit I do enjoy their message. Why? Because I want to LIVE too! I want to make room in my life to live to the very fullest. Ephesians 1:11–12 tells us how: "It's in Christ that we find out who we are and what we are living for. Long before we first heard of Christ and got our hopes up, he had his eye on us, had designs on us for glorious living, part of the overall purpose he is working out in everything and everyone" (MSG). Making room for Christ in our lives, letting him fill every corner, is making room for purpose and hope. That's really living.

How thrilling to know that he has designs on us. He has a well-thought-out plan with each one of his children in mind. There truly is complete, joyous, full blessing in fulfilling his purpose for our lives.

Can you picture your heavenly Father with his eye on you, even before you were born? Can you picture him plucking you out, gently saying, "This child of mine will make a beautiful addition to my kingdom"? You may not always feel beautiful in all the roles he has chosen for you, but each one was tailor-made for you. And when you fulfill them with joy, I believe you are especially gorgeous to your Father.

Jesus reminds us in John 10:10: "My purpose is to give life in all its fullness" (NLT). Imagine being so full of life that there's no room for anything worthless. It's the best kind of "no room"—a fullness that means we have everything we need for a fruitful, joyous life.

Full of the Voice of Gladness

God was readying for the first Christmas before the foundation of the world. We should spend some time readying our hearts. Let's make room in our lives to live in all that fullness he has planned for us. It's a fullness that can spill blessings over to those around us. I've actually seen that happen with my own eyes (not to mention hearing about it from the voices in my head).

But when the fullness of the time had come, God sent forth His Son, born of a woman, born under the law, to redeem those who were under the law, that we might receive the adoption as sons.

And because you are sons, God has sent forth the Spirit of His Son into your hearts, crying out, "Abba, Father!" Therefore you are no longer a slave but a son, and if a son, then an heir of God through Christ.

Galatians 4:4–7 NKJV

What Child Is This?
19
Obedience brings joy

Whose kid is that, anyway?" One of the parents was asking the question at a Christmas party. She pointed at the kid who was pulling shrimp off the hors d'oeuvre tray and flinging them behind the sofa (definitely not a seafood fan). She was about to say something when we both were amazed to see him cram all but one of his fingers in his mouth at once. Pretty impressive. I guess that's how four-year-old boys get rid of fishy-tasting fingers.

When he managed to pull the last three or four fingers out of his mouth, he plunged them into the dip and got in a few good swirls before he dashed over to his mother. He went straight for the skirt of her beautiful silver velvet dress and latched on with his pudgy, dip-covered fingers—all as she was trying to get out the words, "Stop flinging that shrimp!" You have to understand that all this happened at the speed of a four-year-old. It's something like an alternate time reality, only the stains are all too real. I think I heard a sonic boom.

Silver Streak

Although I've never heard anyone specifically say that raspberry dip is not good for silver velvet, I guessed we wouldn't be seeing that silver dress again. Did I mention that the lady who asked the "whose kid" question was the one wearing the raspberry-flavored silver dress? We don't always want to claim them in their most mischievous moments. Her four-year-old was definitely having one of those "spilled some ink on Mommy's rug / made Tommy eat a bug" kind of day.

As a mother of five, I can tell you I've seen worse. I've seen it *all*. Even the cat can dish it out. What's most disturbing about the cat's mischief is that he does it all with that "eyes-half-open" look of rebellion that tells me he's not the least bit repentant.

It's a little annoying, too, that he seems to think all the Christmas celebrating is about him. Sammy seems certain that each year we pull out the Christmas tree for his personal climbing pleasure. The high-hanging breakables work to make the course more interesting for him. I wonder if he's patting himself on the back for scaling the treacherous tree face with no equipment. No harness, no safety helmet—nothing. The animal even works without a net.

You would probably be more impressed with all that if you could see this cat. He's approximately four times his suggested body weight. We like to think of him as a bit of an overachiever, mostly in the food department. He's an overachiever who basically eats, smacks Christmas decorations around, and then takes eighteen-hour naps in various positions all over the house.

Whose Cat Is This?

Sammy does, however, add special activities to his schedule at Christmas. Pouncing on menacing bows and ribbons, for instance, and lying on top of the gift wrap so it can't get away (while we're trying to cut and tape, thank you very much). He also tries to fit his plump body into every gift bag under the tree before the season is finished. Is he trying to find out what the gifts are, or what? I think if he spoke English we wouldn't have a single surprise present.

He recently found a gift bag he particularly liked and decided it would make a nice clubhouse. I don't think he came out of it for a couple of days. It was nice to have a little time off from chasing him out of the tree. I was content to leave him in there. I wonder who let the cat out of the bag.

When he finally came out of hibernation, he must've thought he needed to catch up on his calorie intake. One of the kids was making a sandwich and dropped a slice of bologna. I don't think I've ever seen him move quite that fast. Doesn't he know what that stuff is made of? Later I got busy and left a cup of milk unguarded on a chair in the kitchen. Then I noticed that when Sammy came slowly waltzing into the family room, he had a milk mustache. And that look.

Joy in Obedience

I don't know if Sammy will ever learn the joy of obedience. But I know Mary knew the joy. When the angel told her she would become pregnant, she could've argued. She had to know that this plan would mean that she would be judged wrongly by some people. She had to know she could lose her husband-to-be. She would very likely be mocked and ridiculed. But her answer was, "I am the Lord's servant. . . . May it be to me as you have said" (Luke 1:38).

Her honor and obedience may very well have meant some personal disgrace for her. She was engaged and pregnant. But it resulted in her blessing on a much grander scale. Her obedience meant she could have a part in welcoming the Savior to the world. Her own Savior. And though she may have suffered some humiliation in that day, she is still called blessed all the way to this day. We still read her song of joy in Luke 1. She glorifies the Lord.

Our obedience brings joy too. Jesus said in John 15:9–11, "As the Father has loved me, so have I loved you. Now remain in my love. If you obey my commands, you will remain in my love, just as I have obeyed my Father's commands and remain in his love. I have told you this so that my joy may be in you and that your joy may be complete."

Plugging in to his commands results in joy. It's a joy that is "complete." There's nothing like it.

Sammy? He doesn't know the joy of obedience, but I will say he did find a rapturous temporary joy. He found the shrimp behind the sofa.

And Mary said:

"My soul glorifies the Lord
    and my spirit rejoices in God my Savior,
for he has been mindful
    of the humble state of his servant.
From now on all generations will call me blessed,
    for the Mighty One has done great things for me—
    holy is his name.
His mercy extends to those who fear him,
    from generation to generation.
He has performed mighty deeds with his arm;
    he has scattered those who are proud in their inmost
      thoughts.
He has brought down rulers from their thrones
    but has lifted up the humble.
He has filled the hungry with good things
    but has sent the rich away empty.
He has helped his servant Israel,
    remembering to be merciful
to Abraham and his descendants forever,
    even as he said to our fathers."

Luke 1:46–55

Ding Dong Bells   20
Letting the love of Christ ring in our hearts

*I*t's bad enough when you've just glanced at your Christmas list and you feel that certain gloominess creeping up on you. Instead of hearing Christmas bells, you hear more of a ringing in your ears. And instead of inspiring you to get your Christmas to-do list whittled down, the Christmas ringing inspires you to eat Ding Dongs.

Yes, it's bad enough to glance at your own undone list, but how do you respond when you run into a woman who tells you she finished her alphabetized Christmas list in August and had everything wrapped by September? What do you do when she tells you that most of the gifts are homemade, according to the tastes, hobbies, and birthstones of each person on her list?

I don't have to admit, do I, how intimidated I am by a woman who has check marks on every item on her list and always has her house in order, her car neat and tidy, and a Thigh Master that never gets cold?

Heavy Sighs, Heavy Thighs

All my unchecked lists aside, my house has been in order only a few times (always before company is expected, of course) and my car . . . well, I'll just be honest. Most of the time, my minivan is a rolling compost pile. I found a UFO in there the other day and finally figured out it used to be a banana peel. You can find pictures of it on the cover of the *National Informer*. As for the Thigh Master, one look at these sausages will tell you I don't even own the contraption.

I've decided not to waste time with jealousy, though—even when I run into Mrs. Clean-House-Spotless-Car-Skinny-Thighs. If you happen to run into Thin-Thigh-Girl, maybe you could make a point of rejoicing for her too. Understand that, even with a clean house, a spotless car, and thighs that don't make sparks when she walks, she too faces struggles. Everyone experiences times of trouble—from fluffy thighs to thighs of steel.

Jealousy and envy are joy-robbers that lead to bitterness and all kinds of unhealthy things. When you hear about a woman who, while still finishing her Christmas shopping three months early, gets promoted in her high-paying, high-profile career, do you rejoice for her, or do you go home and eat a box of Ding Dongs?

When you hear about a woman who has a healthy, stable relationship with a supportive, unselfish husband who yearly offers to take half the shopping list and do all of the Christmas baking, are you happy for her? Or do you go home, eat a box of Ding Dongs, and let out a primal scream?

When you hear about a woman who always arrives at church on time with all her children perfectly dressed in their matching seasonal outfits, can you bless her (even if her kids are multilingual, obey her every whim, and do calculus and other higher math tricks on command)? Or instead of blessing her, do you find yourself writing her name out several times in M&M's and eating them one syllable at a time—tucked inside a few double-decker Ding Dongs?

Rejoicing Is Calorie-Free

It's really okay to rejoice in others' successes and blessings. It's even okay to let someone else's successes inspire us. And it's even more okay not to try to *be* someone else. Trying to be Ms. Perfect will likely make us very frustrated. And really grouchy. And we won't even talk about the cellulite build-up from all those Ding Dongs. No Thigh Master could keep up.

Be you. Be thankful to be you. You are a child of God created in his image. He didn't finish making you with an "Oh, I did NOT mean for that to happen!" He planned you. You were on his to-do list when he made you, and I think when he finished, he made a giant check mark with great satisfaction—and great love.

If you'll let your heavenly Father give you even the tiniest glimpse of how much he adores you, you'll be magnificently overwhelmed by his lavish love. You are his precious child. First John 3:1 says, "How great is the love the Father has lavished on us, that we should be called children of God! And that is what we are!"

Rejoicing in the One Who Loves Us

True satisfaction doesn't come from svelte thighs (let there be rejoicing). It doesn't come from a clean house (again I say, rejoice!). True satisfaction doesn't come from what we do or what we have, but it's really all in how much value our Creator has placed on us. He values us and loves us in the most marvelously lavish way.

Why not spend some time enjoying his lavish love for you? That's the kind of message we want to keep ringing in our hearts. It's eternally more satisfying than any M&M/Ding Dong sandwich—with substantially fewer calories.

So, what do you think? With God on our side like this, how can we lose? If God didn't hesitate to put everything on the line for us, embracing our condition and exposing himself to the worst by sending his own Son, is there anything else he wouldn't gladly and freely do for us? And who would dare tangle with God by messing with one of God's chosen? Who would dare even to point a finger? The One who died for us—who was raised to life for us!—is in the presence of God at this very moment sticking up for us. Do you think anyone is going to be able to drive a wedge between us and Christ's love for us? There is no way! Not trouble, not hard times, not hatred, not hunger, not homelessness, not bullying threats, not backstabbing, not even the worst sins listed in Scripture:

They kill us in cold blood because they hate you.

We're sitting ducks; they pick us off one by one.

None of this fazes us because Jesus loves us. I'm absolutely convinced that nothing—nothing living or dead, angelic or demonic, today or tomorrow, high or low, thinkable or unthinkable—absolutely nothing can get between us and God's love because of the way that Jesus our Master has embraced us.

Romans 8:31–39 MSG

Part 5

Giddy-Up, It's Grand

Gripping God's Word

Christmas Baby

21

Growing up is optional, growing in Christ is essential

o the youngsters ever get on your nerves around Christmas? How about the adults who still act like youngsters? Of course, there's a certain kind of growing up that I'm not sure I'm all that anxious to do. There's an undeniable condition I call "Peter Pan Syndrome" that hits me around Christmas. P.P.S. usually starts at the first reminder that I'm one of the grown-ups—and I'm not entirely sure I want to be. Some of us never want to grow up.

I don't think I'm the only one. Many of us experience varying degrees of P.P.S. We would rather get toys than underwear. We want to play with the gifts instead of cleaning up the wrapping paper. We can't seem to get more than a wink or two of sleep the night before Christmas. Of course, when you're a kid, you can't sleep because you're excitedly anticipating morning and all the miniature trains, planes, and automobiles you'll get to play with. When you're an adult, you can't sleep because you're up wrapping last-minute gifts, stuffing stockings, and putting together miniature trains, planes, and automobiles for little people to play with. Funny how growing up changes those things.

What Do You Want to Be When You Grow Up?

Growing up is a lot more than just getting older. It's a lot more than having a different job on Christmas Eve. Ephesians 4:12–13 says to "prepare God's people for works of service, so that the body of Christ may be built up until we all reach unity in the faith and in the knowledge of the Son of God and become mature, attaining to the whole measure of the fullness of Christ." Paul gives us a different take on growing up spiritually when he defines becoming mature as "attaining to the whole measure of the fullness of Christ."

What does a spiritual grown-up look like? Paul tells a little about that too, when he explains a few things about how we'll behave when we have attained to the whole measure of the fullness of Christ: "Then we will no longer be infants, tossed back and forth by the waves, and blown here and there by every wind of teaching and by the cunning and craftiness of men in their deceitful scheming. Instead, speaking the truth in love, we will in all things grow up into him who is the Head, that is, Christ. From him the whole body, joined and held together by every supporting ligament, grows and builds itself up in love, as each part does its work" (vv. 14–16). No longer infants!

Time to Change the Baby

Babies are adorably cute. But adult babies? That's sort of sad. Paul describes spiritual babies as those who don't know what they believe. They buy into whatever weird teaching they heard last. Spiritually immature people believe lies. Sometimes they even perpetuate the lies, spreading deceit right on to the next generation. The sad consequences are long term and widespread.

It's time to leave behind the baby stuff. We need to "grow up into him . . . Christ." Know what you believe and why you believe it. Grown-ups know the truth. Grown-ups speak the truth in love, according to verse

15. And once we know the real truth, we can pass the grown-up legacy on to our children, instead of passing on the lies that are attached to the baby stuff. Paul tells us in verse 16 that grown-ups let Jesus have control and that they are hard workers. They support others and build them up in love. Now that's what I want to be when I grow up!

Baby Food

There are times, though, when it's good to be a baby. First Peter 2:2 says, "Like newborn babies, crave pure spiritual milk, so that by it you may grow up in your salvation." Babies crave what they need. It's not wrong to be a baby. It's just not healthy to stay a baby. Every healthy baby grows.

No need to worry. Growing up "in your salvation" doesn't really affect P.P.S. We might always vote for toys over underwear—and I think that's okay. The most crucial kind of growing up involves getting in on the "spiritual milk" that helps us grow up in our relationship with Jesus. God's Word is sort of the "cow" that provides that milk.

Got Bible?

Through his Word we find out what life is really all about. We find out how trustworthy our God is. We find out how to love others. In Matthew 5:48, Jesus said, "In a word, what I'm saying is, Grow up. You're kingdom subjects. Now live like it. Live out your God-created identity. Live generously and graciously toward others, the way God lives toward you" (MSG).

A mature, loving follower of Christ who stays plugged in to the Word of God knows what and whom he believes, and he knows how to graciously, patiently love like the Father—even when putting together various trains, planes, and automobiles.

No prolonged infancies among us, please. We'll not tolerate babes in the woods, small children who are an easy mark for impostors. God wants us to grow up, to know the whole truth and tell it in love—like Christ in everything. We take our lead from Christ, who is the source of everything we do. He keeps us in step with each other. His very breath and blood flow through us, nourishing us so that we will grow up healthy in God, robust in love.

Ephesians 4:14–16 MSG

Quiet Time in the Loud Season   22
Keeping our time with the Lord in the midst of the busyness

hh, the sounds of the season. Carolers singing, snow crunching, children laughing, bells jingling—Christmas can be a real sound sensation. "Sleigh bells ring, are you listening?" How can you help it? Of course, there are aspects to the season's sounds that may sometimes cause your temples to pound and your right eye to slowly squeeze closed. There comes a point in the holiday when you can't tell if you're hearing sleigh bells or your ears are just ringing again. Creatures are stirring everywhere in this house—loudly.

Where's all the noise coming from? Check these sources:

Top Ten Most Common Sources of Christmas Racket

10. Bell-ringing Santas who try to get the extra donations by hauling in the Super Liberty Ringer 9000
9. Sleigh-scraping noises on the roof—what a clatter!

8. Shopping cart wheels that squeak at such a high pitch that you can hear it long after you've parked the cart (and you're followed by stray dogs for the rest of the afternoon)
7. Carolers with bullhorns
6. Visiting relatives who insist on repeatedly watching the Indiana Jones movies with the surround sound cranked up so high you keep thinking the rolling boulder is coming through your garage
5. The silence-shattering sound of the carpet shampooer sucking up the 1,200 or so stains from the Christmas party
4. The incessant ringing of the phone as your credit card company thanks you again for breaking another company record (Two or three more calls and they'll offer you stock in the company.)
3. The noise-toys your kids got from their grandparents (No one wonders that your parents call these "revenge toys.")
2. Loud people who come a-wassailing (Actually, I have no idea what that is. But I'll bet it's loud.)
1. Grandma getting run over by a reindeer

Add to all that an announcement about a blue light special every few minutes and it can all start to get on your last auditory nerve. The tsunami sound waves can start to drown out some of your holiday cheer. Still, I guess Christmas wasn't built for complete quiet. The first little Christmas lull was followed by a skyful of singing angels. But I can guarantee those were some overwhelming sound waves of glorious sweetness.

So Where's Our Sound Sweetness?

When we feel we're on major sound sensory overload and the season seems the most thunderous in volume and the most engulfing of spirit, what usually gets snuffed out first? Our quiet time! I don't mean time without all the loudness; I'm talking about time alone with the Father. But it's that time with our heavenly Father that can actually quiet our spirits in a way that has nothing to do with the acoustics. Psalm 37:7 says, "Quiet down before God, be prayerful before him" (MSG). Time spent prayerfully reading his message to us, his Word, is time spent quieting, assuring, and sustaining our souls. Even in all the busyness, it's the most important holiday appointment we can keep.

Shopping for people we love, lunch out with a girlfriend, a special job the boss gives us to do—we make time for those things that are most important to us, even when we really don't have the time. We need to understand that there is nothing more important than nurturing and developing our relationship with the Lord by staying linked to him in prayer and listening to him through his Word.

Where Do I Start?

The book of Luke would make a great study at Christmas—or any other time for that matter. Use your Bible study helps and resources; they're great (and there are tons available at your local Christian bookstore). A taste of *White Chocolate* in the morning, for instance, can help you start your day thinking God-ward or help end your day with the sweet sound of Scripture reverberating in your ears—and your heart. You can get a spiritual charge from sources that are sufficiently packed with Bible readings and biblical direction. There's something wonderfully refreshing about his Word. Psalm 119:114 says, "You're my place of quiet retreat; I wait for your Word to renew me" (MSG).

Make sure you choose a source for your quiet time that has God's Word as its central focus. And you never want to totally replace reading the Bible with reading about the Bible. There's nothing like simply picking up God's Word and listening to his unfiltered message to you, the child he adores.

How Sweet the Sound

So even when the sounds of the busy season are echoing at full volume and "Silent Night" is just a song, know that all truly can be calm and bright when we don't turn a deaf ear to his instruction. Keep your quiet time and tune in to God's Word. Read it, study it, memorize it. It's the only place you can find genuinely "sound" teaching.

> I rejoice in following your statutes
> >   as one rejoices in great riches.
> I meditate on your precepts
> >   and consider your ways.
> I delight in your decrees;
> >   I will not neglect your word.
> Do good to your servant, and I will live;
> >   I will obey your word.
> Open my eyes that I may see
> >   wonderful things in your law.
> I am a stranger on earth;
> >   do not hide your commands from me.
> My soul is consumed with longing
> >   for your laws at all times.
> You rebuke the arrogant, who are cursed
> >   and who stray from your commands.
> Remove from me scorn and contempt,
> >   for I keep your statutes.
> Though rulers sit together and slander me,
> >   your servant will meditate on your decrees.
> Your statutes are my delight;
> >   they are my counselors.

                                        Psalm 119:14–24

The Trouble with Cheese Balls 23
Choosing to be washed by the Word

Splish, splash, I was taking a bath / Long before the Christmas Day bash." If only the song could end there. I hate it when I'm getting ready for a big Christmas event and the splish splash becomes a flesh flash. It happens when I get out of the shower and try to wriggle immediately into the control tops. Talk about a sticky situation. I'm tugging at the right leg of the panty hose, but for every inch I lift the stockings, the right thigh flab raises an inch in turn. Have you ever seen a short woman with her thighs around her waist? Let me just tell you it's anything but pretty.

It's a mathematic inevitability: too much flesh plus too little panty hose equals control tops that have a hard time maintaining their control. Control tops (for male readers and/or other non-wearers) are actually the genetic result of a pair of panty hose marrying a girdle and the couple giving birth to an annoyingly high-maintenance child.

The Cheese-Ball Challenge

I wish I could blame it all on the panty hose. But to be painfully honest, there's been too much "Cheese Navidad" on my part. It's amazing to me how a little cheese ball only weighs ten ounces or so, but once inside the body, it converts to at least three pounds. And I don't think I have to tell you what every three pounds does to the panty hose situation. If you can imagine around eight cheese balls sticking over the top of each thigh of the panty hose, you might have a disturbingly accurate picture.

A friend had a suggestion for remedying the situation. She challenged me to say no to a few of those cheese balls. Now that was just crazy talk. Maybe I should give up the showers instead. That could take care of at least part of the control-top conflict. Come to think of it, it would probably take care of all the Christmas event invitations too.

Wash Up

Okay, skipping the showers would stink in every sense of the word. Besides, I hate it when I don't feel clean.

I hate it when I don't feel clean spiritually too. It's the Word of God that does the shower job on our lives, cleansing and renewing our minds. Romans 12:2 says, "Do not conform any longer to the pattern of this world, but be transformed by the renewing of your mind. Then you will be able to test and approve what God's will is—his good, pleasing and perfect will." "Renewing of your mind" happens with the washing of the Word of God.

Our minds are powerful. Never underestimate the power of your thoughts. When your mind is guided by truth and wisdom, life is pleasant, no matter what's happening around you. If your life feels out of control, it's most likely because your mind, your thought life, is out of control. You can have that out-of-control feeling even when circumstances are good, and especially when there are difficulties.

Double Your Displeasure

James 1:8 describes the person who has a mind out of control. "He is a double-minded man, unstable in all he does." Double-mindedness is the foolish way of mixing earthly "wisdom" with the true wisdom that's from God. The mix is about as effective as mixing too many cheese balls with control tops. It just doesn't fit.

The cure for double-mindedness is to let God's Word give us single-mindedness in our purpose. The Lord spells out in his Word our purposes for life and gives us instruction for living. It's the sure fix for the double-minded. Psalm 119:113 says, "I hate double-minded men, but I love your law." Our minds need to be scrubbed clean of the stinky earthly thinking that sneaks into our decision-making processes. As we absorb purpose and instruction from God's Word, we're scrubbing away double-mindedness. James 4:8 says, "Purify your hearts, you double minded."

Is it time for a heart scrubbing? Purifying our hearts is getting rid of sin and rendering our flesh ineffective. Flesh is the carnally thinking part of our minds—our sin nature (never mind the extra cheese-ball flesh).

What Do We Do?

For a renewed single-mindedness, we give our minds the control-top treatment. We girdle it up. "Therefore gird up the loins of your mind, be sober, and rest your hope fully upon the grace that is to be brought to you at the revelation of Jesus Christ" (1 Peter 1:13 NKJV). To "gird up the loins of your mind" is to ready it. The NIV translates the verse this way: "Therefore, prepare your minds for action; be self-controlled."

Read his Word with a readiness to obey. Let it become part of you—part of your thinking. Let it transform your way of doing things. Let it transform *you*. And pray through it. You'll be praying in the will of God. That's when powerful things happen. Keep on asking him to help you fall in love with His Word. That's what I so want for my own life. I want to be consistent in listening to God's Word and the instruction there that can change me.

I think I might listen to that "lay off the cheese balls" counsel too. It could change me around the thigh area.

Blessed are they whose ways are blameless,
  who walk according to the law of the LORD.
Blessed are they who keep his statutes
  and seek him with all their heart.
They do nothing wrong;
  they walk in his ways.
You have laid down precepts
  that are to be fully obeyed.
Oh, that my ways were steadfast
  in obeying your decrees!
Then I would not be put to shame
  when I consider all your commands.
I will praise you with an upright heart
  as I learn your righteous laws.
I will obey your decrees;
  do not utterly forsake me.

                              Psalm 119:1–8

Don't Be a Fruitcake   24
Feeding on truth, not swallowing lies

I 've heard there are people who actually like fruitcake. They don't usually admit to it because of the stigma associated with any kind of fruitcake fancy—not to mention the risk of intense persecution. Fruitcake is ridiculed and parodied through every Christmas holiday season, yet it still bounces back again the next season to offer yet more humor fodder. I use the word "bounce" in its loosest meaning, since I've heard if anyone ever wanted to cut one, it would require a welding torch.

Fruitcake is in fact quite a scientific marvel. It's rumored that there are only about four fruitcakes in the known world and that they're continually being circulated (those gift recyclers at work). Fruitcakes refuse to die. After they've been around the globe a few times, some say they become more geologic in nature. I think scientists and assorted geologists are still conducting extensive research trying to determine if they're animal, vegetable, or mineral. Or none of the above.

Here's a list of practical ideas for those who have received a fruitcake or two, but have never had even the remotest desire to eat one (i.e., most of us):

What Can You Do with Your Fruitcake?

- Fruitcakes make great bookends. I think they keep the bugs away too.
- A fruitcake offers wonderful new ways to threaten your children (as in, "You'd better get that room clean or we'll be having that fruitcake for dinner, mister" or, "Watch your language, young lady, or I'll wash your mouth out with fruitcake!").
- A fruitcake makes a superb doorstop. It holds the door open while you haul in all the gifts you really like.
- It's a helpful step stool to help you reach those higher shelves. For those highest shelves, you can stack several fruitcakes.
- I've heard a fruitcake can become a helpful practice pad for aspiring percussionists.
- A good stack of fruitcakes in the back of a pickup can keep the truck from sliding during those dangerous snow and ice storms.
- Fruitcake makes a very interesting Christmas tree stand. One fruitcake is said to efficiently steady a twelve-foot tree with ease. And it handily matches the trunk.

- The Department of Highways and Transportation is rumored to be conducting tests to see if fruitcakes would be good for filling those pesky winter potholes. I've heard they're also considering lining them up and using them as speed bumps.
- Larger fruitcakes make pretty decent booster seats.
- I've heard they can be used in lieu of sandbags during flood disasters.
- Clever home owners have been seen hiding spare house keys under fruitcakes. Even if burglars suspect the key is there, they won't touch it.
- A fruitcake makes a nice paperweight (though if it's been left growing cultures for too long, it may think you're trying to paper-train it).

Just Say No to Fruitcake

As you may have guessed, I don't do fruitcake — not the consuming or the giving. Ding Dongs are safer all the way around. Please forgive me if I'm offending the fruitcake lovers (all two of them), but some people will swallow anything, won't they?

On a grander scale, there really are people who will swallow anything. They'll believe anything anyone tells them. In all fairness, it can get easy to fall into the world's way of thinking if we're not careful. But it's vital that we learn to spit out the fleshly philosophies.

First John 2:15–17 says, "Do not love the world or anything in the world. If anyone loves the world, the love of the Father is not in him. For everything in the world — the cravings of sinful man, the lust of his eyes and the boasting of what he has and does — comes not from the Father but from the world. The world and its desires pass away, but the man who does the will of God lives forever."

Just Say Yes to Truth

So how do we know "the will of God" that John speaks of here? God's Word! Psalm 119:169 says, "Provide me with the insight that comes only from your Word" (MSG). As a matter of fact, any doubts about the kind of impact the Word of God can have in our lives can be quickly resolved by a tiptoe through the 119th Psalm. Verses 29–35, for example, offer this prayer:

> Barricade the road that goes Nowhere;
>   grace me with your clear revelation.
> I choose the true road to Somewhere,
>   I post your road signs at every curve and corner.
> I grasp and cling to whatever you tell me;
>   GOD, don't let me down!
> I'll run the course you lay out for me
>   if you'll just show me how.
> GOD, teach me lessons for living
>   so I can stay the course.
> Give me insight so I can do what you tell me—
>   my whole life one long, obedient response.
> Guide me down the road of your commandments;
>   I love traveling this freeway! (MSG)

By the way, the "barricade" mentioned here has nothing to do with fruitcake as far as I know—though we shouldn't rule out any possibilities.

I love Psalm 119:129–131: "Every word you give me is a miracle word—how could I help but obey? Break open your words, let the light shine out, let ordinary people see the meaning. Mouth open and panting, I wanted your commands more than anything" (MSG). Desiring his Word with "mouth open and panting" leads to understanding real truth, knowing him better, loving him more, and truly knowing his will. "Break open" his words as the psalmist encouraged, mouth open wide.

Fruitcake? That's different. I would still encourage choosing recycling over the "mouth open" route.

> I have kept my feet from every evil path
> so that I might obey your word.
> I have not departed from your laws,
> for you yourself have taught me.
>
> Psalm 119:101–102

Yuletide and I'm Fried

25

*Where to turn when you're all burned out
with no place to go*

I'm puzzled by that "Twelve Days of Christmas" song. Granted, I am one of those last-minute shoppers. But even with my tendencies to be a major procrastinator, when have I ever experienced a Christmas season that wrapped up in just twelve days? The stores start decking their respective sales halls around twelve days before *Halloween*!

Still, the problem with being Queen of the Procrastinators is that I end up wearing myself to a complete frazzle the last couple of weeks before the big day. I'm dashing here, prancing there—I could be a reindeer! I'm wondering where in the world those nine ladies find time to dance. On the other hand, if "The Twelve Days of Christmas" mentioned nine ladies dashing/prancing, I think I really could gather eight friends and connect to the song in a whole new way.

Five Golden Rings

If my husband is going to connect to the song in any way, however, I try to send him past the long list of fowl and straight to those golden rings. Anything small and sparkly. Now that's probably how they get those nine ladies to dance!

Of course, I could get excited about the eight maids too. Never mind the milking. Around the busiest Christmas times, it would take all eight of those gals to get my house clean. Eight maids a-cleaning! I would be all over that gift even if they didn't do windows.

When I'm doing my own shopping, though, I tend not to take the song's recommendations for gift giving too literally. I don't mean to be rude, but the person who wrote it was one weird shopper. Personally, when I'm shopping for my true love, I steer completely clear of anything that comes in a gaggle. Geese, swans, calling birds, french hens, turtle doves, partridges—what's with all the fowl? You don't suppose the guy is going to ask his true love to fry up some of those birds, do you? Maybe the partridge is hiding in that pear tree so its goose doesn't get cooked. Could we really be singing about three french-*fried* hens?

Fryer Tuckered

I do tend to spend too many dozen days of the season feeling pretty fried myself. It's easy to get tuckered from your head right down to your jingling Christmas socks, isn't it?

Let's see, I need to pick up candy for caroling night, pick up mugs for all the kids' teachers (ugh—another mug year?), pick up cookies for the school party, pick up appetizers for the staff dinner, and pick up decorations for the church party. Then there always seems to be at least one irreplaceable item that's only in stock at a faraway store branch and has to be picked up on a day trip six counties away. After all is said and done (and incidentally, it's never said nor done in just twelve days), I've usually also picked up a big fat headache. Picture me massaging my temples as I deliberate: should I celebrate, decorate, procrastinate, or *medicate*.

Where Can We Pick Up a Little Breather?

Where do we turn when we're all burned out with no place to go (or more accurately, with *too many* places to go)?

We need to go to the Word of God. Before making a shopping trip, a trip through the pages of Scripture can offer just the equipping we need for a day full of hubbub and hullabaloo. Before we pick up anything, we need to pick up God's Word.

Want a real breather? The Bible is God-breathed. Second Timothy 3:14–17 says, "But as for you, continue in what you have learned and have become convinced of, because you know those from whom you learned it, and how from infancy you have known the holy Scriptures, which are able to make you wise for salvation through faith in Christ Jesus. All Scripture is God-breathed and is useful for teaching, rebuking, correcting and training in righteousness, so that the man of God may be thoroughly equipped for every good work."

Pick Up Your Equipment

Thoroughly equipped for every pickup! When we make a spot in the pickup schedule for God's Word, we're letting the Spirit of God equip us for everything we need to do. Not just those physical pickup lists, but the truly important things we need to accomplish. His Word teaches us eternal truths, shows us where we've gotten off track in our focus and our actions, and helps us get back on the right track again. Then it goes even further to help us learn how to stay on that right track and accomplish "the tasks God has for us," as *The Message* puts it. "Every part of Scripture is God-breathed and useful one way or another—showing us truth, exposing our rebellion, correcting our mistakes, training us to live God's way. Through the Word we are put together and shaped up for the tasks God has for us" (2 Tim. 3:16–17 MSG).

I want to be put together and shaped up for the tasks he has for me. Maybe as I let his Word become more and more a part of my life and more a part of the way I get things done, I'll become less and less a procrastinator. Any chance next year we won't see *Procrastinator II*, the terrifying sequel? It could happen—he is a God of miracles!

Either way, I want my twelve-plus days of Christmas to be spent in meditation instead of medication. That's something worthy of contemplating.

I think I still have a little more contemplating to do on "The Twelve Days of Christmas" song. For instance, how can it truly be a Christmas song when they list all those birds, but no turkey?

Let the peace of Christ rule in your hearts, since as members of one body you were called to peace. And be thankful. Let the word of Christ dwell in you richly as you teach and admonish one another with all wisdom, and as you sing psalms, hymns and spiritual songs with gratitude in your hearts to God.

Colossians 3:15–16

Part 6

Do You Hear What I Hear?

Staying in Touch with the Father in Prayer

The Burning Bush

26

Hearing from the Father
without catching anything on fire

I always get so fired up when we're getting ready for one of our ladies' Christmas parties. I remember getting especially fired up for the one we had in my friend Lynn's home a few years ago. Lynn had the whole place stunningly decorated, right down to the pretty candles in the advent centerpiece one of her children had made. We left our finger foods and desserts on the long dining table while the thirty or so women gathered in the great room for prayer.

I noticed while we were praying that one of Lynn's children came and got her and they both quietly slipped out. I could hear Lynn in the dining room softly but excitedly saying, "Oh no, oh no, oh no." At the risk of interfering with one of those motherly moments, I quietly slipped out too to see if I could help.

When I got to the dining room, I found Lynn (still whispering, "Oh no, oh no, oh no") trying to figure out how to put out the lovely centerpiece that had spontaneously combusted into a little campfire. Even when the weather outside is frightful, the fire isn't necessarily so delightful. Not when it's in the middle of the dining table anyway. I grabbed a towel and started batting at it with her, but I think we were literally "fanning the flames."

Blazing New Trails

When I realized we weren't getting anywhere, I did what seemed most logical at the time. I kept batting with the towel, but added hollering. Pretty soon the room was filled with smoke and screaming women. The smoke alarm went off and Lynn's husband came bounding down from upstairs. Our hero. He grabbed the four corners of the tablecloth and picked up our flaming foods in one humongous, Santa-looking bundle. Then he took off running for the front door while Lynn and I put out the leftover flames on her table. Her husband somehow made it to the door without getting burned, then, with everything he had, hurled the blazing bundle out the door.

Strangely enough, it landed right on top of one of their shrubs. It was winter so, while I call it a shrub, it could probably more accurately be described as kindling. It shot up in a bigger inferno than ever. Now what? Gathering hands and circling around it to sing "Kum Ba Ya" didn't seem quite right. We all wondered if her whole house was going to be taken down by one contrary centerpiece.

Lynn's husband looked for the hose, but remembered he had disconnected everything to keep the pipes from freezing. As he was scrambling, my inventive friend, Mary, had already made her way to the kitchen and back. She scooted out the door carrying our huge bowl of punch. Yes, she extinguished the burning bush with fruit juice, sherbet, and a lovely ice ring! You're going to think I made that up just so I would have a good "punch" line, but it's the honest truth.

We all stood there blinking for a minute, looking at the charred bush with our smoking hors d'oeuvres lying around it. There were scattered dessert carcasses everywhere. It looked like someone had decided to make a burnt offering and had given their most precious items. There was chocolate in there, for Pete's sake.

Since no one knew whether to laugh or cry, in the quiet I just announced, "Dinner is served." They decided to laugh. It's a good thing we get a kick out of anything served en flambé.

The Original Burning Bush

In the Bible's original burning bush story, God used the bush en flambé to get Moses's attention. Evidently a tap on the shoulder wouldn't have been nearly as effective. We're told in Exodus 3:2–3 how God "appeared to him in flames of fire from within a bush. Moses saw that though the bush was on fire it did not burn up. So Moses thought, 'I will go over and see this strange sight—why the bush does not burn up.'"

It got his attention, all right. His was a much more unique burning bush experience than mine. I had leftover adrenaline to deal with for several hours. But I'll bet Moses didn't sleep for a week.

Thankfully, we can talk to God with or without flaming vegetation. In fact, I hope I never make him work that hard to get my attention. When the Lord spoke to Moses through the bush, Moses answered in verse 4, "Here I am." He wants our prayerful attention just that way. As a matter of fact, Scripture instructs us in 1 Thessalonians 5:17 to "pray continually." Prayer is our place of connection and our source of power.

Praise, Confession, Thanksgiving, Petition

Praise is an important part of our prayer lives. It's like tapping God on the shoulder for *his* attention. Maybe it's even like sending up a smoke signal. When you pray, praise him for who he is and what he's done. He's all-powerful, all-knowing, all-loving, ever present, perfectly holy . . . and so much more!

As we're praising God for his holiness, our own unholiness becomes painfully obvious. That's a good prayer progression—right into confession. As sin comes to mind, confess it. Toss it out like a flaming tablecloth. Getting rid of sin is oh-so-freeing!

The freedom we feel in his cleansing is cause for great thanksgiving. There's also a huge list of other reasons to be thankful. Our heavenly Father never tires of hearing that list. Thanksgiving should have a prominent place in our prayer time.

God also enjoys our unselfish prayers for others. He even loves to hear us express our own needs to him. He says in James 4:2, "You do not have, because you do not ask God." Go ahead and ask.

You can praise him, confess your sin, thank him, and ask him for your needs and others' needs right now. We do well when we keep a burning passion to pray.

I'll add here that if your burning passion ever leads to any kind of brush fire, Lynn mentioned that being well insured is a very, very good thing. So is having an insurance adjuster with a sense of humor. I think hers is still chuckling.

> Come and listen, all you who fear God;
>   let me tell you what he has done for me.
> I cried out to him with my mouth;
>   his praise was on my tongue.
> If I had cherished sin in my heart,
>   the Lord would not have listened;
> but God has surely listened
>   and heard my voice in prayer.
> Praise be to God,
>   who has not rejected my prayer
>   or withheld his love from me!
>
> Psalm 66:16–20

With a Little Elfin Magic   27
We can cast all our trouble, he's there on the double

Everywhere I turn someone is handing me another cookie. And I just keep eating them. Okay, so I'm not the brightest bulb on the tree. I love sugar cookies in all those cute Christmas shapes and colors. I have no idea how many sparkly green Christmas trees I've consumed since the first of December, but I do believe that if these were real trees there would be rangers hounding me for endangering our national forests.

Do you know what eating a forest of sugar cookies does to a body? Every tree seems to add a little more to my trunk. How can I make all these extra cookie pounds disappear?

I think I'm going to need a little magic. Where's an elf when you need one? Maybe the ones not working with Santa are all baking yet more cookies inside one of those hollow trees. Seems to me if they're the ones making the cookies that turn into cellulite right before my very eyes, they ought to be able to lend a little Christmas elf magic to make the cellulite disappear.

Of course, I'm guessing the elves are already dealing with a few issues of their own. Have you ever asked yourself what kinds of things might irritate an elf? Here's my list (you can check it twice):

Top Ten Things That Tend to Irritate Elves

10. They get less attention than superhero sidekicks, but do so much more work.

9. Not one of them has ever been invited to play college basketball.

8. They do all the work, Santa eats all the cookies.

7. They can never buy pants off the rack.

6. Do you know how far the nearest Starbucks is from the North Pole?

5. I don't think Santa is the one who has to clean the reindeer stalls.

4. No union.

3. Who really *wants* to wear curly shoes?

2. Even with the name similarities, they're hardly ever asked to do Elvis impersonations.

1. Long-distance charges for chatting with U.S. friends could curl your toes — even without the shoes.

No Matter How Far Away You Roam

Happily, when it comes to communication with our heavenly Father, long distance is never an issue. Roaming charges are not a topic of concern either. Anytime, anywhere we have an issue — tiny or huge, elfin or human — we have a Father who cares. He wants us to take every issue to him. Before we call, he's there to answer.

First Peter 5:7 says, "Give all your worries and cares to God, for he cares about what happens to you" (NLT). He says to give him all our worries and cares — all! He truly cares about every heartache, every decision, every worry. Be honest with him, even if your thoughts and feelings aren't too pretty. He knows what you're thinking and feeling anyway. You can't shock your all-knowing God. And he really does want to hear from you. If there's ever a long-distance problem, the problem is not on his end of the line.

Sometimes we let sin creep into our lives. That's what will put a kink in our line of communication. Psalm 66:18 says, "If I had cherished sin in my heart, the Lord would not have listened." Every time we ask for cleansing of sin, he gives it. And every prayer we offer from a cleansed life, he hears.

Hold the Phone

Have you ever been so overwhelmed that you didn't even know what to say to him? Don't worry; he's got that covered too. Romans 8:26–27 says, "In the same way, the Spirit helps us in our weakness. We do not know what we ought to pray for, but the Spirit himself intercedes for us with groans that words cannot express. And he who searches our hearts knows the mind of the Spirit, because the Spirit intercedes for the saints in accordance with God's will." He is there to meet our every need in prayer—even when we're having trouble praying for those needs!

Praying in his power is powerful praying indeed. We're instructed to pray in that Holy Spirit power all the time. "Pray at all times and on every occasion in the power of the Holy Spirit. Stay alert and be persistent in your prayers for all Christians everywhere" (Eph. 6:18 NLT). It's toe-curling power of the nicest kind—without the special shoes.

> Are you hurting? Pray. Do you feel great? Sing. Are you sick? Call the church leaders together to pray and anoint you with oil in the name of the Master. Believing-prayer will heal you, and Jesus will put you on your feet. And if you've sinned, you'll be forgiven—healed inside and out.
>
> Make this your common practice: Confess your sins to each other and pray for each other so that you can live together whole and healed. The prayer of a person living right with God is something powerful to be reckoned with. Elijah, for instance, human just like us, prayed hard that it wouldn't rain, and it didn't—not a drop for three and a half years.

Then he prayed that it would rain, and it did. The showers came and everything started growing again.

James 5:13–18 MSG

The Buying Un-guide   *28*
Un-finding just the right un-gift

inding the perfect gift for the special people in our lives can be quite the challenge. And boy, have I seen some gift disasters! In an effort to guard against more such disasters (and to give this book a practical and seasonal public service property), I thought this would be a good spot to include the "Buying Un-guide"—great ideas for what *not* to buy.

Top Ten Unwanted Christmas Gifts for Women

10. Almost anything that even remotely resembles a power tool
9. Vacuum cleaner bags (even the lavender-scented ones)
8. Car care package, including oil change, tire balancing, and engine additive (no matter how much it boosts performance)
7. Membership to the "Guerilla Weight-loss Center"
6. The special satellite Sports-a-rama package
5. Speedboat power washer
4. *Lethal Weapon* tablecloth with coordinating *Lethal Weapon II* place mats
3. One of those "drink holder with a straw" hats
2. Backyard flea-and-tick treatment
1. Gift certificate to Al's Bait & Tackle

Personally, I could add a few more items to the buying un-guide for myself. I'm a "never buy me anything practical for a gift" kind of gal. I've told my husband when buying for me, he should steer clear of anything with a cord.

And while I confess I'm not the final authority when buying for men, for the sake of balance (having nothing to do with tires), I've come up with some of the more obvious items we would do well to avoid when shopping for them too.

Top Ten Unwanted Christmas Gifts for Men

10. The Basket-Weaving Instruction Trilogy on DVD (not even with the special feature extra footage)
 9. Yet another tie—most men hate wearing the ties they already have
 8. Bunny jammies with feet
 7. Martha Stewart action figure
 6. The book *It's Okay to Cry: Expressing Your Feelings through Exploring Your Emotions*
 5. A gift certificate for leg waxing and a facial
 4. A "How to Enjoy the Shopping Channel" phone seminar
 3. The cute crystal teddy bear figurine you saw at that darling little shop downtown (or anything else with "cute" or "darling" in the description)
 2. A certificate for an all-day shoe-shopping expedition
 1. Anything with lace

When shopping for men, it's usually a good idea to find something with a huge, fluorescent warning label saying that bodily damage is almost surely imminent. If the gift can maim, cause vision loss, or possibly singe off eyebrows, it's got to be a hit. If it comes with a remote, you might see him tear up.

Want to find out what a special someone on your list would really like? Get to know that someone. Ask good questions. It can be easier than you think to find out what gets that person's juices going. The perfect gift may be just a few conversations away. Communication has to be the very best shopper's guide.

Finding Just the Right Gift for Jesus

If you were shopping for Jesus, what do you suppose would make the perfect gift? I know what he wants. He wants you! And he wants you to know him. Just as communication is a great way to find out what to buy a special person on your Christmas shopping list, communication with your heavenly Father is a great way to find out about him. Get to know him. Prayer is our communication. He wants us to spend time with him—quality time.

If there's any un-gift we should make sure we un-give, it's ignoring him. We should always be able to find time to duck away for some time with the most important One of all time—past, present, or future.

Jesus told us we need private times of prayer. He gave us these great how-to instructions in Matthew 6:5–13:

> Also when you pray, you must not be like the hypocrites, for they love to pray standing in the synagogues and on the corners of the streets, that they may be seen by people. Truly I tell you, they have their reward in full already.
>
> But when you pray, go into your [most] private room, and, closing the door, pray to your Father, Who is in secret; and your Father, Who sees in secret, will reward you in the open.
>
> And when you pray, do not heap up phrases (multiply words, repeating the same ones over and over) as the Gentiles do, for they think they will be heard for their much speaking. . . .
>
> Do not be like them, for your Father knows what you need before you ask Him. (AMP)

Then he gave us the Lord's prayer.

Our Father doesn't want to be ignored. He doesn't want just a show of prayer either. He desires sweet, sincere times of communication when we adhere our heart and will to his through experiencing him in a fresh closeness. It's absolutely astounding that when we give that gift of quality time to Jesus, we find it actually becomes an extra-delightful gift for ourselves. It's the ultimate gift!

My Martha Stewart action figure is nodding in agreement.

And when you come before God, don't turn that into a theatrical production either. All these people making a regular show out of their prayers, hoping for stardom! Do you think God sits in a box seat?

Here's what I want you to do: Find a quiet, secluded place so you won't be tempted to role-play before God. Just be there as simply and honestly as you can manage. The focus will shift from you to God, and you will begin to sense his grace.

The world is full of so-called prayer warriors who are prayer-ignorant. They're full of formulas and programs and advice, peddling techniques for getting what you want from God. Don't fall for that nonsense. This is your Father you are dealing with, and he knows better than you what you need. With a God like this loving you, you can pray very simply. Like this:

> *Our Father in heaven,*
> *Reveal who you are.*
> *Set the world right;*
> *Do what's best—*
> *as above, so below.*
> *Keep us alive with three square meals.*
> *Keep us forgiven with you and forgiving others.*
> *Keep us safe from ourselves and the Devil.*
> *You're in charge!*
> *You can do anything you want!*
> *You're ablaze in beauty!*
> *Yes. Yes. Yes.*

In prayer there is a connection between what God does and what you do. You can't get forgiveness from God, for instance, without also forgiving others. If you refuse to do your part, you cut yourself off from God's part.

Matthew 6:5–15 MSG

The Stench That Stole Christmas   29
Making "scents" of it all

I love this particular lady. I really do. I feel it's important to establish that in concrete right off the bat. That said, she came to a Christmas party we had a few years ago and the air is just starting to clear. I never knew a cologne could be so overpowering. If you can imagine a Christmas stink bomb wearing a green sweater, you might be on the right track.

She came in the front door. Her perfume made its own grand entrance about three seconds behind her. Can perfume burn retinas or do any other kind of permanent bodily damage? My eyes started to water from minute one. She gave me a hug, and not only did it just about singe off all my nose hairs, but I started to see stars. It took me a few minutes to decide whether or not I should ask for a little CPR. I checked my pulse—just to make sure I was still ticking. After all, I got quite a toxic lungful of the green sweater. I wouldn't have been surprised if someone told me she had soaked it overnight in a forty-gallon vat of the eau de odor. Surely that sweater had to be flammable. I made a mental note to steer the poor woman clear of any of my candles. Maybe rumors of spontaneous combustion are actually perfume related.

Something's Burning

I opted for sensory battle. Since it was Christmastime, I thought I could get away with burning some Christmas incense to mask the fumes without it seeming too suspicious. I couldn't burn enough incense. And I think she would've suspected something was up if I burned the sweater. I decided there just weren't enough Christmas candles in the solar system to overshadow the stench that nearly stole Christmas. I'm a little ashamed to tell you that I tried to hide from the smell around a corner of the family room, but it "reek-ocheted" off the far wall and almost dropped me like a bag of Christmas fertilizer.

The cologne started to dissipate after a week or so, but my favorite chair carried her aroma until almost spring. I tried some sprays and deodorizers but they didn't do much. I even tried one of those air fresheners that's supposed to take any smell right out of the air, but I think the muscular bouquet of her leftover fumes made it cry. Let's just say her essence was there long after she was gone.

An Air of Prayer

The black plague in fragrance form left a rotten impression in the olfactory department. On the flip side, however, Scripture reminds us of the powerful impression of our sweet-smelling prayers. Our prayers are a fragrant offering to our heavenly Father. Psalm 141:1–2 says, "I pray to you, Lord! Please listen when I pray and hurry to help me. Think of my prayer as sweet-smelling incense, and think of my lifted hands as an evening sacrifice" (CEV). Sweet-smelling incense! Our prayers are sweeter to him than the nicest Christmas potpourri — no cinnamon or pine trees needed.

We're given a hint of the preciousness of our prayer to God in Revelation 5:8 when it speaks of "golden bowls full of incense, which are the prayers of the saints." Can you imagine the Father gathering your every prayer? Can you picture him saving up your prayers in a special place? Can you imagine him going back to them every once in a while and breathing them in again because they are so precious to him? It's like prayer-pourri! I may be taking a few liberties for that visual, but it's certainly no exaggeration to say that our prayer life is enormously important to him and that he cherishes every word spoken to him by the children he adores.

Sense of Prayer

Do you know what else is indescribably marvelous to think about? He delights in hearing our prayers, and he delights in answering them. Would you like to see extraordinarily wonderful things happen in your life? Would you like to experience something bigger than the here and now? Try spending extraordinary time in prayer. He's never surprised or taken aback by anything we tell him or whatever we ask of him. As a matter of fact, since he is timeless, sometimes he's already answering before we know what we're going to pray. He says in Isaiah 65:24, "I will answer them before they even call to me. While they are still talking to me about their needs, I will go ahead and answer their prayers!" (NLT). It makes sweet "scents" when we pray, and it only makes sense to pray!

Not only does he delight in doing what we ask when we ask from a pure heart, but he delights in doing beyond what we can even think up. Ephesians 3:20 speaks of him as the one who "is able to do immeasurably more than all we ask or imagine." Prayer is utterly precious and unimaginably powerful.

Knowing that the Father treasures every prayer and that he's ready to answer before we call can completely change our Christmas atmosphere. It changes how we think, how we respond—it changes us! The more time we spend with him, the more we become like him. It's like having his essence as part of who we are long after we say amen. Now that's a sweet-smelling thought!

I must say it's so much sweeter focusing on the incense of prayer than focusing on that cologne from the place of the dead. I've been wondering if that stuff has done some ozone damage. Don't be surprised if you hear it's being blamed for global warming!

> Yet the LORD longs to be gracious to you;
> > he rises to show you compassion.
> For the LORD is a God of justice.
> > Blessed are all who wait for him!

> O people of Zion, who live in Jerusalem, you will weep no more. How gracious he will be when you cry for help! As soon as he hears, he will answer you.

> Isaiah 30:18–19

Silver Bills   30
When you're ready for a Christmas charge

So much shopping! By the time I finish making my shopping list, I often start to wonder if I'm going to have to sell an internal organ before the bills come in. Incidentally, I'm leery of selling off parts I'm presently using—especially the ones that seem acutely useful. However, there doesn't seem to be a big market for tonsils. Slightly used appendix anyone? Nice spleen—only one owner. How about my gizzard?

I do try to stay this side of the organ black market, but by the end of the shopping season you just might find me turning my purse upside down and giving it several latch-rattling shakes. I don't know why I think I'm going to be pleasantly surprised at what falls out of those dark recesses of my purse. I somehow imagine enough cash to finish off the entire shopping list will suddenly appear—and maybe enough to get my nails done. I'm brought forlornly back to reality when I realize I'll be trying to finish off the list by wheeling and dealing with three nickels, a large ball of purse fuzz, and some stale Juicy Fruit. To say the least, none of that looks good for my nails.

What's in Your Wallet?

I have a feeling I'm not the only one experiencing Christmas budget challenges. I was standing in line at the department store recently, and I'm pretty sure I noticed just ahead of me a neck-high pile of purse fuzz and a giant stack of stale Juicy Fruit packs.

Not sure where to draw your own overspending line? Wondering if you're already ridiculously overspent? Maybe the following list of warning signs will help. By the way, you probably don't need to read them if you've already found yourself standing in front of your own pile of fuzz and fruity gum.

Signs You've Overspent the Holiday Budget

- The check-writing muscles in your fingers are bigger than your biceps.
- Your credit card bill comes in the mail with a certificate for counseling, a free stress test, and a complete heart-health screening coupon stapled to it.
- They name an entire wing of the mall after you.
- You discover you have a repetitive motion wrist injury from swiping your card.
- Your UPS guy sends you his chiropractor bill.

- Your credit card company upgrades you from "silver" status to "moon rock."
- You get thank-you notes in the mail from all of Sam Walton's descendants.
- You hear your spouse with a bullhorn outside your favorite store: "Put down the checkbook and slowly step away."
- You try to use your credit card at the department store and the cashier cranks up a chain saw.
- You tabulate everything you've spent over the holidays and realize you could've purchased a fully equipped tropical island with all the options.

That Rings a Bell

I really don't want buff check-writing fingers to become my norm. I would hate to find myself ringing a bell in front of a kettle with my own name on it. Definitely not the kind of Christmas tune I want ringing in my ears. But, boy, is it easy to overdo it!

Most of us need to plan how much we'll be spending at Christmas, or we'll spend all that and a couple of decimal points more. The next thing we know, instead of hearing the ring of the cash register, we hear the ring of our own kettle bell. Or we might even hear the revving of the chain saw. They're not exactly included in the magical sounds of Christmas.

Of all the most magical sounds, I wonder if our prayer time is one of the sweetest melodies our heavenly Father hears. Whether life is humming along pleasantly or we're suffering through difficulties a lot bigger than a taxing financial situation, prayer should be our continuous response to our God who provides everything we really need. James 5:13 says, "Are any among you suffering? They should keep on praying about it. And those who have reason to be thankful should continually sing praises to the Lord" (NLT).

The temptation is to worry, fret, and stew. But in Philippians 4:6–7, we're instructed to pray instead of worry: "Don't fret or worry. Instead of worrying, pray. Let petitions and praises shape your worries into prayers, letting God know your concerns. Before you know it, a sense of God's wholeness, everything coming together for good, will come and settle you down. It's wonderful what happens when Christ displaces worry at the center of your life" (MSG).

The Christmas Charge

The Christmas charge (a totally non-card-related charge) is to stay connected to our Creator through his provision of prayer. As large as an island, as small as a stick of gum, we are to bring absolutely everything to him—every matter of every size. Mark 11:24 reminds us, "That's why I urge you to pray for absolutely everything, ranging from small to large. Include everything as you embrace this God-life, and you'll get God's everything" (MSG).

The "God's everything" we'll get is not really about all the items on that shopping list. As a matter of fact, it tends to put all those shopping lists in perspective for us. It's about the fruit-filled life he can provide. Galatians 5:22–23 tells what the fruit-filled life includes: "But the fruit of the Spirit is love, joy, peace, patience, kindness, goodness, faithfulness, gentleness and self-control." This is the kind of fruit that will never grow stale. It stacks up eternally better than the gummy kind. And it makes life full, complete—sweet!

So let's stay connected to the Father in prayer and watch as he fills our life with sweetness. You'll find that staying in touch with him also influences every buying decision. I think that means I can keep my spleen. And I found out I don't even have a gizzard.

Our LORD, everything you do
    is kind and thoughtful,
and you are near to everyone
    whose prayers are sincere.
You satisfy the desires
    of all your worshipers,
and you come to save them
    when they ask for help.

Psalm 145:17–19 CEV

Part 7

Hurrah for the Fun, Get the Ministry Done

Serving Up a Great Christmas

O Christmas Tree

Decorating our lives with the beauty of serving

After a few years of marriage, Richie and I knew it was time to finally bite the proverbial bullet and buy a fake Christmas tree. Real trees seemed to be getting more and more expensive every year. We didn't realize how expensive the fake ones were until we did some shopping. I hate it when I have to take out a mortgage to pay for Christmas decor.

We ended up buying an artificial tree anyway, but when we finally found one that would fit in our budget, neither of us was willing to admit the thing looked more like a pot scrubber than it did a tree. I didn't know if I should decorate it or soak it in the sink with the gravy pan. I think if I could've gotten it into a good spin, I could've refinished all my wood floors in record time.

Still, when we put just the right tinsel here and our favorite ornaments there, it was magically transformed into something very close to lovely. Even though the thing was so scratchy I almost wore garden gloves to decorate it, I was always amazed at the festive atmosphere the tree brought into our home. And the bristle scars are finally starting to fade. *"O Christmas Tree, O Christmas Tree, how bristly are your branches."*

Back to the Real Thing

A couple of years with the pot brush and we were back to buying real trees. I couldn't bring myself to throw the fake one away, though. It was the tree that just would not die. While it was really too pitiful to use (Charlie Brown's tree had nothing on this thing), it somehow seemed too good to throw away. Besides, I knew if we ever decided to get a pool, it was sure to make the perfect scourer.

It was nice to get back to a real tree and have the smell of evergreen breezing back into our Christmas surroundings. There were real tree challenges, however, that we'd completely forgotten. For one thing, hauling a piece of forest into the house is no small job. Secondly, I can't figure how the math works, but the surface area changes from the tree lot to the family room. I'm quite sure the Christmas tree is always bigger once you get it home. Why the tree goes through one of those growth spurts once you put it in the car I'll never know. I just decided that we don't really need all that much furniture in the family room anyway. The tree should be enough. Wall-to-wall tree.

Good Ol' Charlie Brown

In other challenges, we never had to struggle to keep the cat from drinking the water out of the stand when we had an artificial tree. We didn't have to vacuum needles either. Not as many anyway. The pot scourer was nothing if not sturdy. But I think pine needles spontaneously generate. Every time I finished cleaning the carpet and put the vacuum away, I'd find yet another pile of needles along the baseboards—even long after the tree was gone! I was still vacuuming needles around spring cleaning time!

Even with all the real-tree challenges, I still get a thrill out of having the real thing—and I can't remember missing the bristle brush much. Okay, I do think of it when I watch the *Charlie Brown Christmas* story.

By the way, I love the part of that Christmas special when Linus comes out and reads the Christmas story—the real thing—from the book of Luke. It reminds me (along with the Peanuts gang) that God was thinking of us that first Christmas. He thought about me when he sent his Son into the world.

That inspires me to think of others. Sometimes I think of our good deeds as being a little like beautiful decorations on a Christmas tree. Just as the right ornaments and trim could transform even our scrub brush of a tree into something lovely, God is able to decorate our lives in beautiful ways when he uses us to minister to others.

Double Beauty, Double Duty

"This service that you perform is not only supplying the needs of God's people but is also overflowing in many expressions of thanks to God. Because of the service by which you have proved yourselves, men will praise God for the obedience that accompanies your confession of the gospel of Christ, and for your generosity in sharing with them and with everyone else. And in their prayers for you their hearts will go out to you, because of the surpassing grace God has given you. Thanks be to God for his indescribable gift!" (2 Cor. 9:12–15).

Paul points out how the Corinthians' service was not only ministering to the people, but that God was receiving extra thanks. Double whammy! Romans 14:18 in *The Message* says it this way: "Your task is to single-mindedly serve Christ. Do that and you'll kill two birds with one stone: pleasing the God above you and proving your worth to the people around you."

Paul reminds us in the passage in 2 Corinthians that our service proves we really do want to be used by God, that the gospel is more than just words, and he even compares their gift of service with the gift God has given by his grace: Jesus! And isn't that exactly what Christmas is all about? Whether you pick the bristle brush or the needle factory, Jesus is the real "real thing" of Christmas.

> Those of us who are strong and able in the faith need to step in and lend a hand to those who falter, and not just do what is most convenient for us. Strength is for service, not status. Each one of us needs to look after the good of the people around us, asking ourselves, "How can I help?"
> That's exactly what Jesus did. He didn't make it easy for himself by avoiding people's troubles, but waded right in and helped out. "I took on the troubles of the troubled," is the way Scripture puts it.
>
> Romans 15:1–3 MSG

Gift Recycling
Recycling gifts of service

32

Does anyone else still have Christmas gifts that have never been used—gifts from Christmas 1983? It's a little guilt inflicting, isn't it? Would any of us admit to Chia heads that remain fuzzless? How about salad shooters that have yet to launch a single veggie? I wonder when someone is going to come up with a Chia-head-shooter. I can picture it growing green veggie hair on Frosty the Snowman, then shooting it out his mouth for a tasty wintry side salad.

Not to add more guilt or anything, but who among us would dare admit how many of our furless pottery heads and dead vegetable bazookas we've slyly slipped into the garage sale bag? If you're a Chia lover or you have a need for a salad bomber, try making the rounds to a few garage sales as soon as summer hits. If nothing else, you could snatch up Chia-shooters galore to give away next Christmas. Some people skip the garage sale middle man and recycle their own unused gifts the next year.

Busted!

Keep in mind that gift recycling can get a little tricky. I have a friend who this year received from her mother-in-law the same Clapper she bought for her the year before. Imagine a Clapper that's been mailed across the country. Twice. That we know of! I think the thing may have more frequent flyer miles than I do! It's the Clapper heard round the world.

And (this is almost the worst) how many of us have opened a gift from a good friend only to find a card inside with someone else's name in the "from" spot and our good friend's name clearly written in the "to" place? How many of us are still good friends with those people?

The Cycle of Life

Still, there really are gifts that are at their absolute best when they're recycled. Each one of us has received a gift of ministry. First Peter 4:10 doesn't leave a single one of us out when it says, "As each one has received a gift, minister it to one another, as good stewards of the manifold grace of God" (NKJV). Each one of us! When we're not recycling those gifts the Father has given us, using them to minister to others, we're not being good stewards of his grace. It's eternally more wasteful than a hairless Chia.

In 2 Timothy 1:7–9 we're told to keep our special gifts of ministry ablaze. "God doesn't want us to be shy with his gifts, but bold and loving and sensible. So don't be embarrassed to speak up for our Master or for me, his prisoner. Take your share of suffering for the Message along with the rest of us. We can only keep on going, after all, by the power of God, who first saved us and then called us to this holy work" (MSG).

Our gifts of ministry are meant to be recycled into service for others by the power of God—even when circumstances are tough. He saved us, he called us to get going in service, and he empowers us to serve. Galatians 5:13 says, "You, my brothers, were called to be free. But do not use your freedom to indulge the sinful nature; rather, serve one another in love." Serving others in his name brings great blessing and unspeakable satisfaction.

Recycling Is People-Friendly

If you haven't been using the gift God has given you to serve others, it's time to dust it off and recycle it. "So let's do it—full of belief, confident that we're presentable inside and out. Let's keep a firm grip on the promises that keep us going. He always keeps his word. Let's see how inventive we can be in encouraging love and helping out, not avoiding worshiping together as some do but spurring each other on, especially as we see the big Day approaching" (Heb. 10:22–25 MSG). You'll be absolutely amazed at the joy you'll find in fulfilling your heavenly Father's plan for you.

As for my plan for this chapter, I think I'm ready to wrap it up. I'll be shutting down my computer now. Clap off!

> Dear friends, do you think you'll get anywhere in this if you learn all the right words but never do anything? Does merely talking about faith indicate that a person really has it? For instance, you come upon an old friend dressed in rags and half-starved and say, "Good morning, friend! Be clothed in Christ! Be filled with the Holy Spirit!" and walk off without providing so much as a coat or a cup of soup—where does that get you? Isn't it obvious that God-talk without God-acts is outrageous nonsense?

I can already hear one of you agreeing by saying, "Sounds good. You take care of the faith department, I'll handle the works department."

Not so fast. You can no more show me your works apart from your faith than I can show you my faith apart from my works. Faith and works, works and faith, fit together hand in glove.

James 2:14–18 MSG

Dressed for the Party   33
Real Christmas dressing

Christmas dressing is really not about a turkey side dish. It's about what to wear, what to wear. I hate it when I'm readying for a big party with lots of glitz and I can find nothing even remotely radiant in my closet. It makes me nervous. If I had Christmas boots, I'd put them on just so I could shake in them.

Surely I should at least be able to find a tiara or something. How else can I feel like the Glam Queen? Admittedly, I'm placing a tall order for a short woman. I want an outfit that makes me look twenty pounds lighter and twenty years younger. Why can't I find anything in my closet to help me with the 20/20 look?

Glimmer Glamour

There is, of course, my glimmer-jacket—a favorite during this season. But how many times can I wear the same glimmer-jacket in the same circle of friends? I so hate to admit this, but I think there are times I would rather wear the jacket inside out than to have too many repeats of the same outfit. Okay, I win this season's Shallow Award.

It's not an award I'm proud of. Especially when I think about what Jesus wore to the first Christmas party. The event of all events—the birth of the Savior of the world—and the Guest of honor wore swaddling clothes.

Jesus lived his entire earthly life clothed in humility. From humble beginnings in swaddling clothes in a cattle-trough-bed, to the servant costume he donned to wash his disciples' feet, to the utter humiliation of the cross—he wore humility on every occasion.

What to Wear, What to Wear

We're instructed to dress accordingly—to humble ourselves according to his example. We tend to want a "manager" position instead of a "manger" position. But if we want to humble ourselves as our Master did, we need to make sure we're never a manger stranger. To wear swaddling clothes in a cattle trough, to put on a servant costume, to wear the attire of the cross—that's what it is to wear Christ. Colossians 3:12 says, "Therefore, as God's chosen people, holy and dearly loved, clothe yourselves with compassion, kindness, humility, gentleness and patience."

We're given the message again in 1 Peter 5:5 when it says, "All of you, clothe yourselves with humility toward one another, because, 'God opposes the proud but gives grace to the humble.'" Humility! That's what the best-dressed servant of God is called to wear!

Crowning Glory

It all painfully boils down to the fact that it doesn't matter if I wear the jacket inside out or upside down. I'm not called to be crowned the Glam Queen. I'm called to humility and service, sacrificing myself for others. First Peter 5:2–6 says,

Just as shepherds watch over their sheep, you must watch over everyone
God has placed in your care. Do it willingly in order to please God,
and not simply because you think you must. Let it be something you
want to do, instead of something you do merely to make money. Don't
be bossy to those people who are in your care, but set an example for
them. Then when Christ the Chief Shepherd returns, you will be given
a crown that will never lose its glory. All of you young people should
obey your elders. In fact, everyone should be humble toward everyone
else. The Scriptures say, "God opposes proud people, but he helps
everyone who is humble." Be humble in the presence of God's mighty
power, and he will honor you when the time comes. (CEV)

Excuse me, did that say I would be given a crown? Yes! A tiara of my
own! And yet I'm compelled to remember that anything tiara-worthy
I'll ever do in this life will only be as a result of the Spirit of Christ
working through me. I love the Revelation 4:10–11 picture of falling
down in worship, laying our crowns before the One and Only Worthy
One: "And they lay their crowns before the throne and say, 'You are
worthy, O Lord our God, to receive glory and honor and power'"
(NLT). No cubic zirconia in this crowd! These are our offerings to
the God who deserves all glory.

Getting Ready

Getting ready for the chic party of the year doesn't compare to the
party of all parties when Jesus comes to gather us home. And Jesus
instructs us to be ready for his coming by clothing ourselves in humility
and servanthood. He says in Luke 12:35, "Be dressed ready for service."
When we comprehend that dressing for humble service means we're
dressed in a way that pleases our Master, then we're not blinded by the
glitter and we can see life's big picture so much more clearly.

Hallelujah, it's real 20/20 vision!

Don't push your way to the front; don't sweet-talk your way to the top. Put yourself aside, and help others get ahead. Don't be obsessed with getting your own advantage. Forget yourselves long enough to lend a helping hand.

Think of yourselves the way Christ Jesus thought of himself. He had equal status with God but didn't think so much of himself that he had to cling to the advantages of that status no matter what. Not at all. When the time came, he set aside the privileges of deity and took on the status of a slave, became human! Having become human, he stayed human. It was an incredibly humbling process. He didn't claim special privileges. Instead, he lived a selfless, obedient life and then died a selfless, obedient death—and the worst kind of death at that: a crucifixion.

Because of that obedience, God lifted him high and honored him far beyond anyone or anything, ever, so that all created beings in heaven and on earth—even those long ago dead and buried—will bow in worship before this Jesus Christ, and call out in praise that he is the Master of all, to the glorious honor of God the Father.

Philippians 2:3–11 MSG

Gift Giving Made Queasy

34

De-Grinching your Christmas

I try to read every book and article on gift giving made easy that I can get my hands on around this time of year. I found another one just the other day. But it seemed to me that particular author's version of "easy" would not only require a Ph.D. in several areas of study, it would also take a withdrawal from the National Treasury to make it all happen. The "simple" craft projects were filled with instructions to fold, spindle, and mutilate—but all I could grasp was the mutilating. I couldn't find one project in the whole lot that was anywhere near my idea of easy. In fact, they all made my head spin and my stomach hurt.

When crafting won't cut it, it's back to the mall. Again. On one of my recent shopping trips, my stomach was queasy before I even made it into the first store. The parking lot alone was enough to send a fragile stomach into months of meds. I waged one ugly battle with an SUV vying for the only spot on the entire south lot of the mall. We were at equal distances from the coveted parking spot. She was coming east, I was heading west—it was like shoppers' chicken. I decided sometime after that day that I would be doing the rest of my Christmas shopping in a tank, thank you. Want a piece of *this*, SUV?

When I finally parked the car and hiked the forty-some-odd miles to the entrance (needless to say, I lost to the SUV), I accidentally got in some sort of mosh pit where parents were waiting for a store clerk to pass out the new shipment of the electronic toy of the hour. It was like being in a giant blender preparing to make a massive shopper smoothie. Claustrophobes were doomed.

I saw two shoppers getting to know each other much better than they ever intended. They were smashed together, face to face. One said, "Did you know you're breathing on me?" then added, in a lovely display of holiday spirit, "Spearmint gum?"

Giving without the Humbugs

While you might find more spearmint than Christmas spirit in the holiday shopping blender, most of us do think about giving during the holiday season like no other time of year. We may run into an occasional Grinch and a few scattered Scrooges, but on the average, folks are in the giving spirit.

I think it must please the Lord when we honor his birthday with benevolence. A mature believer is one who gives generously and cheerfully. Second Corinthians 9:6–7 says, "Remember this: Whoever sows sparingly will also reap sparingly, and whoever sows generously will also reap generously. Each man should give what he has decided in his heart to give, not reluctantly or under compulsion, for God loves a cheerful giver."

"Exchanging" gifts is the Christmas norm. Real "giving" happens when we're not exchanging or trading gifts but giving to someone who can't give back. And we're instructed not to give out of guilt or because someone makes us feel like we have to but to give with careful thought and with joyful exuberance.

Penny-Pinching Prison

Should gift giving really be made "easy"? In truth, sacrifice is an extraordinarily precious thing. Sacrifice and generosity are even freeing. Scrooge-ishness, on the other hand, is a prison. When we are selfish, stingy, and tight-fisted, we put ourselves in service to money, not God. And when we serve money, we become its slave. Jesus said, "You cannot serve both God and Money" (Matt. 6:24). The entire passage makes it clear that loving and serving money is blinding. We completely lose sight of the big picture. Suddenly our eyes are zeroing in on temporary material things and we miss the light of God.

Giving gifts to everyone else and forgetting the one with the birthday would make for a warped celebration. Can I issue a challenge to make the biggest gift this year to Jesus? It's his birthday! Maybe he'll lead you to make the gift to your church. Maybe he'll lead you to give in the form of a missions offering, a special anonymous gift to someone in need or to an organization that furthers his kingdom. Maybe it will be a gift of time or service. Maybe all of the above! It's a great feeling!

The Heart of Christmas

While we get a nice feeling from giving, our motivation should be wrapped up in more than just the giving tingle. It should certainly be about more than just a couple of last-minute tax write-offs. Real gifts come from the heart.

Giving heart-gifts is the result of . . . well . . . giving your heart as a gift. It's the very best gift to give your Savior on his birthday. How much of your money does he really want? All. He also wants all your time. All your resources. All of YOU. He can use our all—even when it seems very small—to make something humongously beautiful. The gifts we give to others are not measured in amounts. God measures at the heart level. Are we giving from a pure heart of love and generosity, or are we giving to impress someone? Out of duty or out of love?

Remember as you're giving that you won't find anywhere in Scripture the command to give more than you have. Debt isn't in his plan for your giving. He wants us to share what he's already provided. After telling us that God loves a cheerful giver, 2 Corinthians 9:8 says, "God can bless you with everything you need, and you will always have more than enough to do all kinds of good things for others" (CEV).

Give heart-giving a try. You may find yourself positively bowled over with the blessing it sends back your way. Bowled over with blessings—not breath.

> Tell those rich in this world's wealth to quit being so full of themselves and so obsessed with money, which is here today and gone tomorrow. Tell them to go after God, who piles on all the riches we could ever manage—to do good, to be rich in helping others, to be extravagantly generous. If they do that, they'll build a treasury that will last, gaining life that is truly life.
>
> 1 Timothy 6:17–19 MSG

Go Shine It on the Mountain   *35*
Sharing Christmas glitter

I bought a new glittery dress this year. I'm such a sucker for a shiny getup. I could hardly wait for a Christmas event dressy enough to warrant pulling out the glitzy new frock. I sorted through the invitations and found one that said "semi-formal." Close enough! I was so ready to sparkle!

And sparkle I did. Everywhere I went. Every time I moved or gestured in any way, a flurry of glitter would flutter all around me. I'm sure some people thought they were watching the special effects in a *Star Trek* scene: "Beam me up, Scottie!" Every time I moved to a new mingle spot in the room, not only could I look back to find I'd left behind a shimmering lake of glitter, but then I would watch in alarm as I started a whole new glassy sea in my new spot. I found glitter everywhere I stood—glitter on my chair, glitter stuck to my face, glitter leeching my husband. I think I may have even accidentally eaten some. I needed a twinkle toothpick before the party was over. I'm sure I was shining inside and out.

Can you imagine how surprising it is to find your favorite Christmas dress is molting? At least I could never lose my way while wearing the sparkly dress. I could just do the Hansel and Gretel thing and follow the glitter crumb trail back home.

If only they had been seeds. I was scattering enough twinkly kernels to grow several acres of glitter plants. I could start my own glitz farm! Several acres of glitter plants and a few sequin bushes and I could harvest an entire Oscar event or two. Of course, on that farm I'd need a diamond tree. I kind of like the sound of that. E-I-E-I-O.

Ready to Shine

I need to always be ready to sparkle—no matter what I'm wearing. Christmas is the perfect time to share the real gift of Christmas with friends and family. Sharing the gift is sharing the good news that Jesus Christ was born. It's sharing that by his birth, death, and resurrection, he provided a way of salvation for all who give their hearts and lives to him.

So many people are already celebrating his birth in the holy season—even though they may not know exactly what his birth means for all people and for them personally. We can let them in on what it means—and what it can mean for their eternity. It's the light Jesus has given us to share. He said in Matthew 5:14–15, "You are the light of the world—like a city on a mountain, glowing in the night for all to see. Don't hide your light under a basket! Instead, put it on a stand and let it shine for all" (NLT). Jesus wants us to shine the wonderful, glittery message of salvation from the mountaintop. Hide our sparkle? Unthinkable! We should be shining inside and out.

Shine It, Tell It

Psalm 9:11 says, "Tell his stories to everyone you meet" (MSG). Tell it on the mountain. Tell it at the party. Tell it at the mall. Tell it! Every time we tell it, we're planting seeds for the harvest. Actually, it's quite like having a glitter farm—except the harvest doesn't outfit the stars for any particular awards ceremony on this earth. The harvest is the very souls of people, letting them know they can be outfitted for heaven!

Jesus said in John 4:35–36, "Look around you! Vast fields are ripening all around us and are ready now for the harvest. The harvesters are paid good wages, and the fruit they harvest is people brought to eternal life. What joy awaits both the planter and the harvester alike!"

(NLT). Getting to have a part in the harvest to end all harvests brings a joy that will glisten throughout eternity. You can't find a better wage for any kind of farm—never mind the *e*'s, *i*'s, and *o*'s.

Leave a Shining Trail

So many people are walking in darkness. They've lost their way home. We need to leave evidence of the light everywhere we go so that others can follow the shining trail to Jesus. Glittering bread crumbs that lead to our eternal home! We have the harvest words of Jesus in Matthew 9:37–38: "Then he said to his disciples, 'The harvest is plentiful but the workers are few. Ask the Lord of the harvest, therefore, to send out workers into his harvest field.'" What a privilege it is to serve as one of his workers.

I want to keep on shining. Not with the dress. I want to shine with the message of salvation through Christ. It's incomparably more rewarding than any earth-glitter. And it never gets stuck between your teeth.

> You are the light of the world. A city on a hill cannot be hidden. Neither do people light a lamp and put it under a bowl. Instead they put it on its stand, and it gives light to everyone in the house. In the same way, let your light shine before men, that they may see your good deeds and praise your Father in heaven.
>
> Matthew 5:14–16

Part 8

Do You Recall the Most Famous One of All?

Remembering Jesus
as the Reason for the Season

Candy Cane Christmas

36

Jesus is the answer to every mystery

I had the cutest candy canes hanging on my tree a few years ago — tons of the adorable little things. So delightful I decided to store them for use the next Christmas. But when I went to get them out of the basement the next year, they were gone. What's really weird is that when I looked in the box I was sure I stored them in, all I found was the most bizarre UFO-looking thing I had ever seen. Well, not that I've seen any UFOs, but let me just say that Spielberg would've loved this thing. It was about the size of a basketball with little spikes sticking out of it everywhere that gave it a bit of an eerie celestial look. It was white with flecks of red here and there, and it smelled a little minty. I wondered for a minute if the thing had eaten my candy canes.

I made the mistake of picking it up out of curiosity, and you'll never believe what it did. It grabbed me back—sort of adhering itself to my fingers! I thought I was about to be assimilated. It didn't take control of my brain or anything, but it was so sticky it took me several minutes to disengage.

Eventually I did figure out what had happened. That's when I came up with a helpful hint for many Christmases to come: never store peppermint candy in a basement if there's a chance your air conditioner might be down for a day or two in the summer. The star blob was actually all my Christmas tree candy canes stuck together in a giant spiky mint-orb. That hot summer day with no air conditioner had melted the stripes right off of them and bonded all of them into one mega-mint. Once I put it all together, the UFO was no longer a mystery. Weird and a little disgusting, but not mysterious.

Other Assorted Mysteries

There are other mysteries we're still working on. At my house it's always a mystery exactly who pinched all the chocolates in the Brach's box. It's also a mystery to me why anyone would choose to drink eggnog.

It's always a mystery how our Christmas season will unfold. It's a mystery how our entire lives will turn out, for that matter. So many questions, so few people who'll tell you where to find the answers. Isn't it completely bewildering what some people do when they're looking for answers to life's questions? What do you do when you're looking for life instructions? Ask your average Joe-searcher how to find answers in life and this is what you might get:

The Top Ten Average Ways to Find the Answers to Life

10. Send a letter to Santa—or at least Dr. Phil.

9. Since reading tea leaves is tough to do with instant or bagged tea, some try reading the bubbles in their Holiday French Vanilla Cappuccino instead.

8. Watch reruns of *Star Trek: Deep Space Nine* until all the answers to all of life's questions in this particular space/time continuum become clear.

7. Since animals know things, write out all your possible life choices and show them to your dog. Stay away from the ones he buries.

6. See if you can make out ancient hieroglyphs in the family room carpet fibers. The ones written with Sesame Street markers don't count.

5. Surely your life questions were all addressed on *Full House*. They talked about everything. Fortunately it's on at any hour in any time zone.

4. Check with *American Idol's* Randy, Paula, and Simon. If Simon has something positive to say, surely it has to be right.

3. Examine the cat fur on the living room rug. Is there a subliminal message? (Disregard if the message reads, "You live to serve the cat.")

2. Try interpreting the patterns in the candy cane stripes (if they're not all in one chunk).

And the number one average way to find the answers to life?

Surf the Internet.

Sadly, most of us have probably tried something similar to at least one of those average ways to find answers. I don't know about you, but I don't want to settle for average.

Where do we find above-average ways to get the answers to life? Above! Colossians 3:1 says, "Since, then, you have been raised with Christ, set your hearts on things above." As Christians who have been given a resurrected life in Christ, we need to find our answers for life in him. Verse 2 says, "Set your minds on things above, not on earthly things."

Striving to Be Seriously above Average

The earthly way of doing things is extremely below average. *The Message* puts Colossians 3:1–2 this way: "So if you're serious about living this new resurrection life with Christ, act like it. Pursue the things over which Christ presides. Don't shuffle along, eyes to the ground, absorbed with the things right in front of you. Look up, and be alert to what is going on around Christ—that's where the action is. See things from his perspective."

The answers to life are found in Christ. He spells out our instructions for living and for knowing him in searching his Word, not in cat fur or coffee bubbles. Keep looking above. Jesus is the reason for every season. He's our reason for living, and our lives should ever and always be all about him. No matter what Simon says.

> This is GOD's Message, the God who made earth, made it livable and lasting, known everywhere as GOD. "Call to me and I will answer you. I'll tell you marvelous and wondrous things that you could never figure out on your own."
>
> Jeremiah 33:2–3 MSG

Settled Down for a Long Winter's Sugar Coma   37
Jesus's birth, death, and resurrection settles everything

I figured it was probably time to go on the current season's healthy eating kick. How did I know it was time? I called them "little sugar cravings," but when I caught myself shooting out of the car after a morning of shopping and landing almost instantly at the pantry door, I figured I'd probably already let the sugarfest go on for too long. I was like a treat-seeking missile—with a chocolate target. When it gets that severe, the Christmas candy is doomed. Not even the chocolate chips are safe. Picture me huddled in a corner of the kitchen, hiding the bag, waiting for the insulin shock to settle in. Talk about a long winter's nap.

It's also a clue that it's time to rethink the sugar binge status when I choose which party to attend by ranking the goodies. "Jane tends to serve all that healthy veggie stuff. Let's go to the Maxwells'. Mrs. Maxwell covers all her cookies with fudge." There's an even bigger red flag when I find myself choosing a Sunday school class by rating their doughnuts. "She's a good teacher, but she only serves glazed. Linda's class always brings those chocolate-covered, custard-filled long johns." It's hard to compete with a fudgy coating. It's especially hard to beat a really good long john.

I guess the real clincher is when I catch myself digging through the toes of the kids' Christmas stockings for any leftover chocolate snowmen. That's especially a dead giveaway if I find snowmen from five or six Christmases ago—and I still eat them.

Examining the Evidence

Every now and then, I have to examine my sugar passion to make sure I'm not so out of balance that I outgrow all my clothes. Who wants to have to wear a Christmas *tent* to the Maxwells' party?

I sort of examine my own evidence and testify against myself. Do I have to admit how many times I've had to find myself guilty? Pleading "not guilty on account of undue sucrose influence" doesn't cut it. I'm busted! If I've tackled a couple of my kids for the last Ho Ho, for instance, I don't have much choice but to send myself to calorie prison. Bang the gavel. That settles it.

It's Settled!

I'm so glad Jesus settled the truly big issues. We never have to wonder about his love for us. It's eternally more intense than any choco-need I'll ever experience. He proved his immense, unconditional, unshakable love when he came to earth in human form, then died on the cross—all to make it possible for us to have a right and tight relationship with him. But if you examine the evidence (never mind the Ho Ho's), you'll find that he went all out to prove his power to save. The same power that saves us from sin raised him from the dead. Now that settles it!

How glorious that Jesus didn't stay a baby in a manger. He didn't even stay in the grave. We can serve a risen, LIVING Savior! Romans 8:11 says, "It stands to reason, doesn't it, that if the alive-and-present God who raised Jesus from the dead moves into your life, he'll do the same thing in you that he did in Jesus, bringing you alive to himself? When God lives and breathes in you (and he does, as surely as he did in Jesus), you are delivered from that dead life. With his Spirit living in you, your body will be as alive as Christ's!" (MSG).

Living Power

Because Jesus is alive, we've been made spiritually alive. We have so much to celebrate at Christmas. Jesus settled it all by his astounding birth, through his incomparable sacrificial death, and in the earth-rocking event of his resurrection.

There's power in the living, resurrected Savior to resist temptation—chocolate and otherwise. There's power for living. Romans 6:8–11 says, "Now if we died with Christ, we believe that we shall also live with Him, knowing that Christ, having been raised from the dead, dies no more. Death no longer has dominion over Him. For the death that He died, He died to sin once for all; but the life that He lives, He lives to God. Likewise you also, reckon yourselves to be dead indeed to sin, but alive to God in Christ Jesus our Lord" (NKJV).

Christmas should be a season of remembering. I love remembering and celebrating the love-driven, earth-changing, life-giving, sin-conquering, resurrection-proven power of the living Christ of Christmas. It's one more reminder that every eternal issue has been settled once and for all. There's soul rest in that kind of remembering.

By the way, soul rest isn't related in any way to sugar-induced naps. It's a completely different rest. Soul rest happens when we remember that Christ settled it all. A sugar-induced nap? That happens when we eat through the toes of the kids' stockings.

> As for you, you were dead in your transgressions and sins, in which you used to live when you followed the ways of this world and of the ruler of the kingdom of the air, the spirit who is now at work in those who are disobedient. All of us also lived among them at one time, gratifying the cravings of our sinful nature and following its desires and thoughts. Like the rest, we were by nature objects of wrath. But because of his great love for us, God, who is rich in mercy, made us alive with Christ even when we were dead in transgressions—it is by grace you have been saved. And God raised us up with Christ and seated us with him in the heavenly realms in Christ Jesus, in order that in the coming ages he might show the incomparable riches of his grace, expressed in his kindness to us in Christ Jesus.
>
> Ephesians 2:1–7

The Skinny on Christmas 38
Remembering our Savior's willingness to put on skin

Have I ever mentioned what a terrible memory I have? Maybe it slipped my mind. I bought all the vitamins that are supposed to help with memory, but I keep forgetting to take the little rascals. Most people remember either names or faces.

Some really sharp cookies remember both. Most of the time I remember neither. It's so embarrassing to be at a Christmas party and suddenly realize you know the names of only a third of the people there—and they're all family! I've always wished I had a photographic memory. Someone told me I actually do have one—it's just not developed. I always seem to be a few snaps short of a full roll.

Get the Full Meal Picture

My brain is such an interesting piece of contradictory gray matter. It struggles to find the matching name file for most face files, but it zips an immediate neural message for every happening that involves food. All synapses are firing when there's a nice dinner involved.

It's funny that I never forget a lunch date. I never forget the Christmas parties with the tastiest goodies. Come to think of it, I never forget any meal at all. Sometimes I remember meals that aren't really supposed to be meals—though I'm able to conveniently forget how many sausage rolls I've eaten. And while I've faithfully made it to each meal, the last three days in a row I've made it all the way to the end of each day without remembering to work out. I was supposed to spend at least a half hour a day on the elliptical machine (which looks sadly more like a spastical machine when I'm on it, but that's a topic to tackle another day—if I remember). I have a feeling I'll remember all too well that I forgot to exercise when I try to slip into my party dress this weekend. Sometimes my "selective remembering" really hurts.

Choosing to Remember

I never want to be selective, however, about remembering the God of my Christmas and the glorious things he has done. While remembering him doesn't necessarily do much for my physical muscle, it's a great exercise for building obedience muscle. Deuteronomy 4:9 says, "Only be careful, and watch yourselves closely so that you do not forget the things your eyes have seen or let them slip from your heart as long as you live. Teach them to your children and to their children after them."

These instructions to Israel are instructions for us too. Forgetting was easy for them, and sadly, it's still easy today. *The Message* puts verse 9 this way: "Just make sure you stay alert. Keep close watch over yourselves." Remembering the things he has done has a purifying effect on our lives. We need to "stay alert" and to "keep close watch" over the things in our lives that would distract us from what he wants us to do.

Meals, exercise programs, and lots of those temporary things will come and go, but Deuteronomy 4:23 says that we have to "be careful not to forget the covenant of the LORD." I want to be careful to ever remember the Name of my awesome God—even if I can't remember the name of my first cousin, "What's-His-Face."

God in Skin

The real skinny on Christmas has nothing to do with how many Christmas sausage rolls I eat or how many imaginary laps I take on the exercise machine. It's all about remembering the Savior who put on skin and came in a human body, for me. And for you.

John 1:14 says that "the Word [Jesus] became flesh and made his dwelling among us. We have seen his glory, the glory of the One and Only, who came from the Father, full of grace and truth."

God in the flesh led to God on a cross, and so was born our salvation. Jesus left a beautiful heaven and all his rights as God to become a human. He came to die on the cross to pay for our sins. Remembering why he came is remembering what Christmas really is.

I want to remember to give every part of my gray matter to him, every part of my heart, everything from the skin in—even if I never remember how many of those sausage rolls I've eaten.

Remember that Christ came as a servant to the Jews to show that God is true to the promises he made to their ancestors. And he came so the Gentiles might also give glory to God for his mercies to them. That is what the psalmist meant when he wrote:

> "I will praise you among the Gentiles;
>   I will sing praises to your name."

And in another place it is written,

> "Rejoice, O you Gentiles,
>   along with his people, the Jews."

And yet again,

> "Praise the Lord, all you Gentiles;
>   praise him, all you people of the earth."

And the prophet Isaiah said,

> "The heir to David's throne will come,
>   and he will rule over the Gentiles.
>   They will place their hopes on him."

So I pray that God, who gives you hope, will keep you happy and full of peace as you believe in him. May you overflow with hope through the power of the Holy Spirit.

Romans 15:8–13 NLT

Oh, Fudge! 39
The sweetness of a God-honoring holiday season

I really am dreaming of some white chocolate. And what about the fudge! Oh, the fudge! It's one of those holiday delights we choco-lovers look forward to every year. Fannie Mae? Love the girl. Ooh, and I love sampling from Whitman's. After all, I'm just following directions. Doesn't it say to "sample" right on the box? And have I ever told you that if my husband had let me, I would've named one of my children Ghirardelli?

I never cease to be amazed—and particularly thrilled—at the new things people come up with to cover with chocolate each year. Chocolate-covered pretzels, chocolate-covered peanut butter balls, chocolate-covered *chocolate*—chocolate-covered everything! I think it's wonderfully holly-jolly that Christmas tends to be the most fudge-coated holiday of the year.

Holly Jolly Jelly Belly

I may have already mentioned that, come January, Santa's belly isn't the only one shaking like a bowl full of jelly. Mine is less jelly, though—more chocolate cream. I'm thinking of having a Hawaiian-style Christmas. If I could do anything I wanted, I would just don a muumuu and get back to the fudge. I guess when I think it through, it's a good thing I can't do anything I want.

We tend to want everything that's wrong for us. The curse of sin does that. How amazing it is that Jesus can change our sin condition.

He exchanges our sin for his own righteousness. And then he gives us a new "wanter." Philippians 2:13 says, "For it is God who works in you both to will and to do for His good pleasure" (NKJV). He takes care of both the "willing" and the "doing." Not only does he empower us to do what we need to do, he gives us the want to. He's the One at work inside us through the indwelling presence of the Holy Spirit. He's the One who causes our lives to be fruitful, to be filled with good works.

And I can't think of anything I love more (not even chocolate) than the idea of bringing him good pleasure. You know what's remarkable to me? When I'm bringing him pleasure, it gives me great pleasure too! It's about as sweet as chocolate-covered chocolate. Give us the sweetness of honoring God as he works in our lives!

Joseph's Honor

When I think of Joseph, I think of a man who was committed to honoring God. He was pledged to Mary—it was engagement with an extra kick. While they weren't living together, their betrothal was as legally binding as marriage. The only way to break the engagement was divorce. They were committed to each other. I can hardly imagine how he must've felt when he found that the sweet girl he had so dedicated himself to was pregnant. It had to feel like a kick in the stomach.

Under Jewish law, he had every right to make her humiliation public and have her stoned. But Matthew 1:19 tells us that Joseph was a "righteous man." His righteousness made him a man of mercy. So it says, "Because Joseph her husband was a righteous man and did not want to expose her to public disgrace, he had in mind to divorce her quietly." His heart must have been breaking.

I can picture the heartbroken Joseph tossing and turning in his bed, finally making up his mind what he would do, then slipping off into a troubled sleep. That's when a shocking message from an angel in a dream changed everything. The angel told Joseph that it was okay to take Mary as his wife and that her baby was conceived by the Holy Spirit. This was to be the Savior—Immanuel, God with us!

So what did Joseph do? He woke up from his dream and did exactly what he was told. I don't know if he even considered what he "wanted" to do. He wanted to honor what the Lord wanted. Can you imagine what pleasure Joseph's obedience and honor brought to his heavenly Father?

Honor the Father

People find new and creative ways to celebrate the birth of Christ. Some are good. Some are just plain weird. I like what Joseph did. He simply obeyed and honored God.

I've noticed that a lot of the ways people celebrate Christmas involve finding new and creative uses for chocolate and condensed milk and marshmallow creme. And of course, the Cool Whip possibilities are almost endless. But me? Give me Jesus first and foremost. Give me the will to obey and honor. And if it's okay to add this somewhere down the list, give me chocolate too.

> This is how the birth of Jesus Christ came about: His mother Mary was pledged to be married to Joseph, but before they came together, she was found to be with child through the Holy Spirit. Because Joseph her husband was a righteous man and did not want to expose her to public disgrace, he had in mind to divorce her quietly.
>
> But after he had considered this, an angel of the Lord appeared to him in a dream and said, "Joseph son of David, do not be afraid to take Mary home as your wife, because what is conceived in her is from the Holy Spirit. She will give birth to a son, and you are to give him the name Jesus, because he will save his people from their sins."
>
> All this took place to fulfill what the Lord had said through the prophet: "The virgin will be with child and will give birth to a son, and they will call him Immanuel"—which means, "God with us."

When Joseph woke up, he did what the angel of the Lord had commanded him and took Mary home as his wife. But he had no union with her until she gave birth to a son. And he gave him the name Jesus.

Matthew 1:18–25

Come and Behold Him

40

Meet Christ the Lord this Christmas

I have such a creative pastor/husband. He's never afraid to try something new. One year for the Christmas Eve service, for instance, he decided to let people in on what it was really like that very first Christmas. The church auditorium took on a stable feel. After covering the platform with plastic, he brought in real hay. And then he brought in sheep. Real sheep.

My kids volunteered to be shepherds. Andrew, Jordan, Kaley, Allie, and Daniel were all decked out in their cutest shepherding duds (motherly speaking). I don't think they knew what they were in for. Jordan's sheep charge was a real bruiser. There were a couple of times when it looked like a "ba-a-ad" WWF moment. (That's World Wrestling Federation for those of you fortunate enough not to know.) I watched nervously worrying that at any moment the thing would get Jordan in a headlock.

The sheep were squirming, making unmentionable messes (that part was not exactly my idea of "worshipful") and interrupting the music like you wouldn't believe. By the way, sheep have no sense of rhythm and they do NOT sing on key. The whole thing was like a rather outrageous jungle scene. I thought our church should consider adopting a new slogan for our Christmas Eve service: "We put the 'native' in 'Nativity.'"

Kaley's sheep kept trying to escape. He fidgeted and wriggled until finally one of his hooves came down solidly on her toe. She was trying not to make a big scene—after all, the sheep was making a plenty huge scene already, but she said it really smarted in the worst way. She got through it by keeping her mind busy. She was toying with the idea of reinstating animal sacrifices.

The Sacrifice to End All Sacrifices

Ever wonder why they had those animal sacrifices in the Old Testament? Every sacrifice in the Old Testament was to atone for sin—and every one pointed toward the cross. At Christmas we celebrate more than the baby in the manger. Because he was God, Jesus grew up living a perfect life and ultimately became the once-and-for-all supreme sacrifice on that cross.

Hebrews 9 compares the old sacrificial system to the new covenant we have in Christ. We're told that the priests were able to go in and out of the outer place of the tabernacle as they performed their duties. But only the high priest was able to go into the Most Holy Place. Before he could do that, he had to offer the blood of animals to cover his sins and the sins of the people. Verse 9 says, "This also has a meaning for today. It shows that we cannot make our consciences clear by offering gifts and sacrifices" (CEV).

How amazing is the good news of this passage that Christ has now become our High Priest. "Once for all time he [Christ] took blood into that Most Holy Place, but not the blood of goats and calves. He took his own blood, and with it he secured our salvation forever" (v. 12 NLT).

Our salvation has been bought and paid for by the precious blood sacrifice of the one and only Son of God. John 3:16 and 18 says, "This is how much God loved the world: He gave his Son, his one and only Son. And this is why: so that no one need be destroyed; by believing in him, anyone can have a whole and lasting life. . . . Anyone who trusts in him is acquitted" (MSG).

Stable Forever

We can have a stable relationship with our Holy God. Not stable as in "give the church sanctuary a barn feel," but stable as in everlastingly unshakable because of the Savior of the world. Salvation was God's firm plan long before that first Christmas. Isaiah 53:5–6 prophesied the Messiah's sacrificial death: "But he was pierced for our transgressions, he was crushed for our iniquities; the punishment that brought us peace was upon him, and by his wounds we are healed. We all, like sheep, have gone astray, each of us has turned to his own way; and the Lord has laid on him the iniquity of us all."

Like sheep gone astray? We've all been there! We've in essence stomped on the very toes of God. That's what sin does—though on a vastly bigger scale than WWF. Our God is so holy our minds can't fully comprehend it. In his holiness, he can't have fellowship with sin. We've each one turned our own way—opposite God's way. Without a perfect Savior to pay for our sin, we're all doomed to an eternity separated from him.

But God in his mercy made new life available to us in his new covenant sealed by the blood of Jesus. Jesus is like the Kiss of God. He is the heavenly mistletoe for all humankind.

How about You?

I'm guessing the majority of folks who've made it to this page of *White Chocolate* already have a deep and loving relationship with the Father. If that includes you, I'm rejoicing that we're forever siblings. Even if we never meet in this life, we're sure to get to chat in Glory.

And I know if you're his child, you don't mind reading the salvation story again. It just gets sweeter, doesn't it?

Maybe you're new to the faith. Welcome! Or maybe you made a decision to give your life to Christ some time ago, but you've somehow drifted away from following him. It's no accident you picked up this book. God has a beautifully orchestrated plan for your life. Now is the time for you to surrender yourself completely to the Christ of Christmas.

If you've never accepted Christ as your Savior, this could be the very point in time when your destiny changes forever. You can settle your eternity no matter where you are or what you're doing. Pray something like this from your heart with all sincerity:

> Father, I know I've chosen my own way instead of yours. I've sinned against you, O Holy God. Thank you for sending your only Son to pay for my sin with his own blood—the sacrifice to end all sacrifices. Please forgive me through that blood sacrifice. I believe that Jesus died for me and rose again, conquering sin and death once and for all. I trust you right now to cleanse my every sin, to make me clean and new. Thank you for loving me. I give my life and my all to you. I'll serve you with everything I have and everything I am with every day you give me from this moment forward. May my life bring glory to you. Thank you for saving me. In Jesus's name, Amen.

If you just prayed that kind of prayer for the first time, your life is now under the new covenant—you've been radically and eternally changed. It's a life free from the eternal death sentence of sin. "Because of the sacrifice of the Messiah, his blood poured out on the altar of the Cross, we're a free people—free of penalties and punishments chalked up by all our misdeeds. And not just barely free, either. Abundantly free!" (Eph. 1:7 MSG).

What a great adventure you have in store! Let me be the first to wish you a truly Merry Christmas—the kind with Christ right where he should be: at the heart. The Lamb of God has taken away your sin, as promised.

Merry Christmas to All . . .

My wish for you all, friends, is that Jesus will guide your every step through your Christmas and throughout your life. May your days be merry and bright, and may all your Christmases have plenty of white chocolate.

> Under the old system, the blood of goats and bulls and the ashes of a young cow could cleanse people's bodies from ritual defilement. Just think how much more the blood of Christ will purify our hearts from deeds that lead to death so that we can worship the living God. For by the power of the eternal Spirit, Christ offered himself to God as a perfect sacrifice for our sins. That is why he is the one who mediates the new covenant between God and people, so that all who are invited can receive the eternal inheritance God has promised them. For Christ died to set them free from the penalty of the sins they had committed under that first covenant.
>
> Hebrews 9:13–15 NLT

Rhonda Rhea is a humor columnist and has written numerous articles for *HomeLife*, *Today's Christian Woman*, *Marriage Partnership*, *ParentLife*, and many other publications. Also a radio personality, she is a frequent guest of Focus on the Family's *Audio Journal*. She is the author of *Who Put the Cat in the Fridge? Turkey Soup for the Soul*, and *Amusing Grace*. Rhonda and her husband, Richie, live in Troy, Missouri, with their five children.

Visit her website at www.RhondaRhea.net.